FOOTBALL INSIDE OUT

FOOTBALL
INSIDE OUT

ALAN GOWLING

SOUVENIR PRESS

ISBN 0 285 62307 9

Printed in Great Britain by
Bristol Typesetting Co. Ltd,
Barton Manor, St Philips, Bristol

Contents

Pictures by courtesy of the Newcastle Chronicle and Journal, Daily Mail, Trievnor Simpson, Capital Press Photo, Topix, Sporting Pics., (U.K.) Ltd., Jim Appleby

1 The Devil and the Deep Blue Sea

'There are not many careers where the rate of failure is as high as that in football.'

This was one of the comments I made when I wrote a thesis about Soccer, during the time I was taking my Master of Arts degree. My experience in professional football, embracing clubs in the First, Second and Third divisions of the League, enables me to say now that I see no reason to revise that impression. Indeed, there was a stage in my own career where I had practically decided to give up the game, and go into the world of business. At that time, I was experiencing all that was worst as a professional . . . playing for a club which had dropped from the First to the Second to the Third Division, and was in imminent danger of descending into the Fourth. It was at that stage that I made up my mind: no way will I slide into further obscurity – I'll quit the game first.

And it was just then, when my fortunes were at their lowest ebb, that I was given a lifeline, the chance to haul myself up into the First Division again, in one swift, overnight move. I snatched at the chance because I believed I had something still to offer, at the highest level in the game, and I proved it to my own satisfaction.

Now, as I look back at those sombre days of near-despair, I am thankful that I did get the chance to play First Division football again, and – thinking of many other professionals who have been far less lucky than myself – I often think: 'There, but for the grace of God . . .' For football is a game where you must have not only ability and the will to succeed; you must also have some luck on your side. Given the combination of these three factors, you can hope to get to the top.

Before we go any further, let me say that this story is not intended to be a learned exposition, weighted with long words which few people can understand. Having been a professional footballer for several years, I know as many earthy words as any guy on the shop floor of the factory, and I've used plenty of expletives in the heat of the moment, whether it's been on the training pitch or in the thick of the action on match days.

Players are a peculiar breed. When things are going well, they are on top of the world. When things go wrong, they worry and it shows. It's the same with teams. And managers. In times of high tension, you'll hear players saying of the manager: 'I don't think he knows which way to turn,' or 'Clutching at straws . . . that's what HE's doing.' Sometimes, the criticisms – whether of manager, coach or directors – will be bordering on revolt. The players will question the whole aspect of management, be highly critical of team selection (especially if they're the ones left out), and you'll hear remarks like this.

'He's supposed to be a track-suit manager – but we hardly ever effing see him!"

Or: 'How can we expect to win matches away from home, when he only plays two effing forwards up front?'

I recall an occasion when the players of a team began to question the tactics which were laid down. Results away had not run in the team's favour, so they began to criticise the manager's persistence in employing a 4-2-4 formation away from home, while the opposition was playing 4-3-3.

The reaction: 'How the hell can we cope, when they have an extra man in midfield, and they're running all over us?' And this questioning attitude very definitely led to a deterioration in the players' relationship with the manager.

Success is what governs people's views of managers, teams and clubs. And players, of course. Every youngster who leaves school set on becoming a professional footballer has dreams of playing at Wembley, winning medals – and, perhaps, in the process, of making his fortune. And to a lad about to embark on a career in professional football, the successful club will look more of a proposition than one half-way down the table. I know one youngster who had two choices: he could have signed for a club close to his home (and he had a lot of respect for that club), or he could join one considerably further afield, which had a far greater history of success. He chose the more successful club.

You join a professional club because someone – manager or scout, for instance – has spotted you playing, and likes what he sees. The process is extremely selective, because there are always more lads with ideas about breaking in than there are places for them to break into. And even then, when a club signs a lad as an apprentice, it takes a gamble that he will eventually make the grade. There is no way of knowing whether or not a lad will achieve his full potential. One youngster is tenacious, has bags of confidence, reads situations well, but lacks ball control; another has skill in abundance, but doesn't read the game well at all. Either or both might make it – or fall by the wayside.

I have never pretended to be one of the game's glamour boys. I know my limitations. My game is based on what I believe is considerable skill, an intelligent appreciation of what is going on around me on the field of play, and – whatever imperfections I might have – absolutely 100 per cent willingness to work throughout the 90 minutes of the match. I'm tall, lean, and a glutton for work. In my days with Manchester United, I was once termed 'The Galloping Chip'.

In my school days, I played on opposite sides to Steve Heighway, who found fame with Liverpool. Steve played for Moseley Hall Grammar School and I played for Stockport School. Now and again, our paths have crossed since those days, as we have moved in First Division circles. Steve has collected winner's medals with Liverpool in the F.A. Cup, the European and U.E.F.A. Cups, and the First Division; I've been to Wembley and finished on the losing side with Newcastle United in the League Cup.

Like Brian Hall and Steve Heighway, I combined a university course with professional football – and at one stage, the pressures of this exacting double role almost led to my having a nervous breakdown. When Hall, Heighway and Gowling began to make their names in professional football, it was suggested that this was the dawn of an era where more and more scholastic types would become stars in professional football. I didn't believe it would happen, and it never materialised.

I had ambitions to become a professional footballer when I was eight years old. I certainly didn't think then that I was going to achieve those ambitions by taking a university degree. My father used to spend a lot of time kicking a ball around with me in the garden, and I simply thought of myself as an embryo professional Soccer player.

I was naturally right-footed, so my father kept on making me practise using my left foot. And in between times when we were kicking a ball around, we used to watch the professionals in action, at Maine-road. So I became a Manchester City fanatic. Indeed, I would never have considered going to watch Manchester United play at

Old Trafford then, and it was ironic, perhaps, that later United were the club for whom I did sign professional.

I watched Manchester City play for the first time when I was about six or seven – it was a birthday treat when my father took me to see them, and we viewed the game from the stand. Later, playing out on the park, I learned that when you're close to the fans on the terraces, you can become very much aware of the caustic comments which are sometimes directed – and there are times when you are the target for their abuse.

That day at Maine-road, as I sat at the back of the stand, with the roof blurring the vision a bit, I thrilled to the spectacle of the men in blue playing against Arsenal. This was the City team which, for the main part, had won the FA Cup in the mid-1950's, and the names of Bert Trautmann, Ken Barnes, Dave Ewing and Bobby Johnstone were very much in my mind and close to my heart. Closest of all was Trautmann – the blond giant of a goalkeeper was my idol. Later, in the days when he had been transferred from Huddersfield to City for a then staggering amount of money, Denis Law superceded Trautmann as my favourite player. Little did I realise that one day, I would play for the same club as Denis . . . or that I would move to Huddersfield, and sample what being one of Soccer's poor relations was like.

In his days at City, Denis seemed to do everything and be everywhere. He wasn't just the king of goal-poachers; he was a forward, a defender, a midfield player – everything rolled into one. He was my idea of the complete footballer.

Not surprisingly, I day-dreamed of becoming another Denis Law – and all the time, my father kept on helping me to improve my football skills, while impressing on me also, at every opportunity, that a professional Soccer player's life was a short one, and that it was important to stick to my schooling, so that I could achieve a standard academically which would give me a chance of security outside the game, should I ever become involved with it at professional level.

I played for Stockport Boys, for the Cheshire Under-15 and Under-18 sides, and for the English Grammar Schools side. I went to a national school Soccer festival, and – in my third season with Cheshire – was selected for two sides to play against the young talent of Arsenal and West Ham. Then I got into the squad to play against Scotland, at Under-18 level, and it was during this time that I came into contact with a young man who was later destined to make a name for himself as the team manager of Wales. He is, of course, Mike Smith, who at that time was in charge of the England Under-18 side.

I admired him then as I do now. I played in midfield, and his ideas coincided with mine about the job I should be doing. Mike's idea was that you passed the ball square only as a last resort; when you gained possession, you should immediately be looking to pass the ball forward, or go forward with it yourself. Passing the ball square was synonymous with passing the buck to a team-mate.

I scored when I played for the England Under-18 side against Wales at Coventry, and we won 3–0; I scored again when we played Scotland at Ibrox and won 5–1. And I 'scored' with Manchester United, as well, because by that time, I was going down to Old Trafford for training two nights a week. Joe Armstrong, who was such a father figure on the scouting side at United, invited me to go along and show what I could do.

As a diehard Manchester City supporter still, I was taken aback when I met Joe Armstrong for the first time, and realised that he was offering me a chance to sample football with the opposition. But he was very persuasive, and it wasn't long before he had me going along to meet Matt Busby, who was managing United then. Despite my Manchester City devotion, I had admired Busby, and once I had chatted to him for a short time, there seemed to be nothing for it but to go down to Old Trafford two nights a week and during the holidays. City had signally failed to show any interest in me, although I knew that apart from United, Everton, Bolton, Bristol City, Portsmouth and Stockport County – my home-town club – all had ideas about signing me.

But Manchester United fitted in better with my ideas of how I wanted to plan the next few years of my life. They seemed to be particularly understanding and sympathetic to my ambitions of taking 'O' and 'A' levels, and while they wanted me first to sign associated schoolboy forms, and then become an apprentice, there was no undue pressure put upon me. In fact, they encouraged me to pursue my studies and, if things went well for me, to go to university.

Perhaps here it's worth looking a bit more closely at what life is like for an apprentice footballer who has joined a club straight from school at 16, because I was one of the privileged few, if you like, who in the end had the best of both worlds. A club is allowed a maximum of 15 apprentices, although this doesn't mean that it always has 15 young Soccer hopefuls on the books. The process, while inevitably a gamble, is as selective as possible, and the bigger clubs, also inevitably, tend to skim off the cream of the young talent.

Normally, the bigger, more successful clubs sign players who have already shown that they have real potential, because of their outstanding ability which has seen them already chosen for their county or their country. A lad will have been watched closely while he is still at school, and once he has finished his formal education he signs apprentice professional. That's when he also finds himself in the cold, cruel world that is professional football – because, immediately, he is competing against other youngsters of his age, and it can be a cut-throat business.

The working hours of apprentices are divided between training and playing games, and doing chores from cleaning boots to cleaning out the dressing-rooms. In fact, there are occasions when the apprentices could consider themselves to be like 'fags' at public school, as they cater to the whims of the 'real' professionals, who can be pretty strict in their demands concerning boots and kit.

During training, there are times when the senior players and the apprentices are invloved together, and on these occasions the apprentices are expected to push themselves harder . . . so they come in for a mixture of encouragement and abuse. When the apprentices train on their own, it can be even tougher, because then they are in direct competition with lads of their own age, and the rivalry may be intense. For right the way through, the apprentices know they are still very much on trial.

They are being tested, and they are testing themselves. Attitude and character come into it – and fear. The fear being that if an apprentice doesn't make the grade, he will find the club releasing him when his apprenticeship has ended, that at 18 he can literally be on the scrapheap, with no training for another job, even though there is a scheme designed to enable him to learn a trade, alongside his Soccer career.

The very real problem – the heart of the problem – is that a lad wants nothing more than to graduate as a professional footballer. So he may tend to 'skive', when he is supposed to be learning another trade. His whole ambition is wrapped up in kicking a ball around, and he is desperately anxious not to slip in this direction, desperately anxious that his fellow-apprentices don't steal a march on him.

Apprentices want nothing more than to become 'real' professionals, and they don't take long to ape those who have already made the grade. The apprentice learns the footballer's language and terminology, learns the tricks of the professional and copies his style. Conform in these respects, thinks the apprentice, and you're half-way home. At the same time, try to get too close to being the 'real thing', and you'll find that you're coming in for rough treatment, physically during training, and verbally, as well. Get too cocky, and the senior players will swiftly cut you down to size, and make you realise that your place is still on the bottom rung of the ladder.

I remember a club tour during which the players thought one apprentice was becoming to cocky for his own good. At the same time, they reckoned that because he was on tour with the senior players, he might become even more big-headed. So, during five-a-side games, he was the butt for sarcastic remarks, with every mistake he made being harped upon. By the end of these sessions, the lad's confidence was shattered, and he was making bad passes galore, and even mistakes when there was no pressure on him from opponents.

The professionals – by which I mean the established players – don't like to see apprentices making them slog it out too much, either, in training sessions. During running, for instance, an over-enthusiastic apprentice will find himself being cajoled by his betters into settling to their pace, instead of going flat out and making them step up their own efforts. The senior men are well aware that they are pacing themselves so that they are in peak form for the next match, which is the supremely important thing. On their display then can rest their first-team fate.

Yet the apprentice is between the devil and the deep blue sea. While his seniors are telling him that there's no need to kick during a practice match ('Saturday's what matters . . . and if it moves then, kick hell out of it'), the coaches will be encouraging the apprentice to get stuck in – and the youngster himself is acutely aware that his future at the club depends on how he survives with the professionals. At times, if a lad fails to conform with the ideas of the established professionals, there can be open clashes of temper, and even fights.

So the young apprentice – who cannot compete at all with his seniors in one respect (the money they earn) – has to mature very quickly in life, because he is subjected to constant pressures from a variety of people, and above all, he knows the price of failure . . . he's out of the game and having to fend for himself as best he can elsewhere. One young player summed it up like this: 'I promised to go to day release course, for my mam and dad's sake. But while I was at college, I found my mind wandering . . . I was thinking about the other apprentices, wondering what they were doing. I was wondering if I was missing something that would give them an advantage over me. After all, football is THE most important thing. That's the career I want, more than anything.'

So it's a case of let your rivals steal a match on you, and you may suffer; show too much enthusiasm during training with the senior professionals, and they'll be yelling, 'Steady on! Cool it . . . there's a bloody long way to go yet . . .' And all the time, the coaches are at you to put in 100 per cent, and then some.

In one way, I was spared the torment of mind that many apprentices must go through, as they wait and weigh up their chances of signing full-time professional forms. In another way, I suffered just as keenly, because I was trying to combine two exacting jobs. I didn't sign apprentice forms, but as I continued my studies, I continued to go to Old Trafford two nights a week for training. By the time I was 18, it was clear that I was coming to the crossroads, though.

I went to Cambridge University for an interview, but the idea of leaving football for a full-time academic course never really appealed to me, in spite of the fact that my headmaster thought I was daft. In the end, indeed, he met my father and myself, and it was only then that he was convinced I was deciding for myself which course I wanted to take. I think he felt that my father was the guiding force behind my insistence that I wanted to combine studies and Soccer – until, at that 'summit' meeting, I spelled it out that I was making my own decision.

By the time I was 18, then, with 'O' and 'A' levels behind me, I had gained a place at Manchester University, and I was happy that this would enable me to keep going down to Old Trafford. I had played for the school in a morning, and for one of the United's junior sides in the afternoon, and got to both games because my father or one of the masters, Malcolm Fidgeon, ensured that they were there with transport.

Malcolm, a qualified FA coach, later became a scout for Manchester United. While he was teaching, I learned a lot from him about Soccer, and I realised, among other things, that he could put his views on coaching across in a manner that was easily understood by players at school level. One of the criticisms the anti-coaching brigade make is that coaches talk in terms which convey little and mean less. Malcolm was and is down to earth, and you could take in what he told you.

I remained an amateur player when I started my second 'career' at Manchester University. And on the footballing side, I was still acquiring experience of the professional scene with Manchester United. One week was outstanding for me – on the Monday night, I scored seven goals for United's B team, on the Wednesday I hit a hat-trick for the A team, on the Saturday I made my debut for the reserves against Preston, and scored the equaliser in a 1–1 draw.

All of which suggested that I was making progress in Soccer, as well as going for a degree at university, so I had every reason to hope that I would be able to achieve success in both fields. And in that respect, I had a considerable advantage over the average apprentice, who knew that he had to bust a gut to make the grade in professional football, or there was precious little for him to fall back upon, other than the first job he could land outside the game, should he fail to convince his coaches and manager.

Even so, I didn't appreciate that it was going to be a real sweat for me, before I had finished, or that my footballing career would take one or two curves – downward, as well as upward – before I would be able to say: 'Yes, I played alongside George Best, Denis Law, Bobby Charlton, Malcolm Macdonald – and scored more goals than 'Supermac' did, in a season.'

2   Stand-in for a Star

'Once you sign professional, the enjoyment goes out of the game. There's too much pressure for you to enjoy it like you did at school.'

That's been the lament of more than one man who found that it was hard going, making a living from professional football. Another put it this way: 'I get paid for something I enjoy doing, but I don't enjoy it as much as I did. The higher I've got in football, the less I seem to have enjoyed it. The pressures of success spoil the fruits of success.'

So, if Soccer can have that effect upon a player, who would be a manager? – Dozens and hundreds of people . . . including those who have never kicked a football professionally in their lives. Yet they still believe they could be successful as the manager of a football club. My first experience of a manager was Matt Busby, as he was then, and no one came under greater pressure than he did, during his managerial career. Yet he managed to combat the pressures, stay sane, and always – well, almost always – appear to be actually enjoying the job.

More often than not, the manager has been a professional player and experienced the trials and tribulations of the players under him. More than anyone else in the club, he knows their problems. With such an advantage, it might seem natural that his relationship with the players should be a good one; but this does not always follow. For, as a manager, the ex-player finds he requires skills different to those when he was manipulating a football. Now, he is manipulating people. And that poses problems.

Initially, he may start his managerial job with enthusiastic ideas about tactics, coaching, and the type of player or players he requires in his side. Almost overnight, he comes up against two problems: the fact that players have differing personalities, and the fact that the club may be on a tight purse string (no matter how eagerly the promise was made, when he took over, that 'the money will be found for the right men.')

Once a manager forsakes the players' world, he is identified in their eyes as an extension of the club. Indeed, he becomes the personification of that institution. Suddenly, he alone is responsible for results – and he is a genius, if he can persuade his board of directors otherwise, when things have gone sadly awry. Too much failure, and he finds himself out of a job; and he knows (even if the players don't stop to think too much about it) that on the field, the players alone can hold the key to the manager's future. Further, he is in no position to do anything about it, once the ball has started rolling.

The manager may have laid down the tactics, but in the heat of the action, players forget what they have been told. So all it needs on the part of even one or two players is indifference on the field . . . and the manager can be sliding on a greasy pole towards unemployment. The manager tries his utmost to weld a team; but each player in the side has his own personality. And that makes for problems, too.

The manager can tell the individual the role he wants him to play, the tactics he wants him to employ. He can initiate set-pieces calculated to produce goals or prevent goals. All this is fine, during the training sessions. The manager has to give his players the belief that everything he is doing is for their own good – whether it's advising them about finance, fining them for contravening the club's rules, telling them to get their hair cut, or even imposing restrictions on their sex life.

The manager has to earn respect, without familiarity. He cannot be seen to have favourites, although everyone knows that, human nature being what it is, a manager must like some players better, as persons and as foot-ballers, than others. The manager can never get too close to the players, but he has to try to be a father to them. And there is, inevitably, a clash of expectations between the manager and the players.

The manager must view matters from the standpoint of the team; the player sees only his own interest and, there-fore, expects to be treated by the manager in that interest. The player often expects from the manager what he is not prepared to (or cannot) give; and, at the same time, a manager is not always truthful with a player. If a manager shows a lack of respect for a player's intelligence, the player will reciprocate this feeling. Such an instance oc-curred at a club where the manager, recently installed, told a player that if he got himself fit, he would have a chance of a place in the side.

Within a fortnight the manager had called the player in again, this time to say he had no chance of a place, and was for sale. The player, amazed and disillusioned, summed up his feelings: 'The club will shit on you, if you let them."

There was the case of a manager who led his team to a commanding position in the league table, yet never quite managed to gain the full respect of his players. Even-tually, the situation took a turn for the worse, and the lack of respect by the players became evident. It's when the pressures and tensions of the game – lack of results, or loss of a first-team place – begin to apply that the manager-player relationship can be all but destroyed.

The most potentially explosive relationship is that where the player is on the fringe of the first team, but never becomes a regular. The manager recognises the player's disappointment, but expects him to accept the situation and strive just as hard as before; the player sees the manager as someone who is thwarting his ambitions, and it will be easy for him to watch first-team men retaining their places, week after week, and claim that they are playing badly. They may be playing badly, too, at that.

There was the day of a local derby game, and one side had several players doubtful, because of injury, so the manager named a large squad to turn up for the match. Going off normal practice, one player assumed that he would be in the team, if the 'regular' failed his fitness test. The night before the game, however, a reserve match was played, and the manager took off a player who was having a good match, in order to put him into the first team the following afternoon. When the player who had expected to be chosen arrived at the ground, he found himself out of the side, and he was blazing. 'The boss is a rat! The little bastard!' was his reaction.

When you are a player at one of the big glamour clubs, the competition for places is that much more intense, and the stars may even block the route to promotion for youngsters, who can lose heart. Even when you get into the first team, you may have to contend with problems.

I became a regular reserve at Manchester United, playing at centre-forward, and Don Givens was my main partner for several seasons. I enjoyed playing alongside him, and we struck up a good partnership – it was almost like the Kevin Keegan-John Toshack partnership at Liverpool. Don always had talent, in my opinion, but he got only a handful of first-team games, and I didn't really feel he got the breaks. The time came when United had a bit of a clear-out, and Don went to Luton Town, along with full-back Peter Woods. Around the same time, Luton also signed players such as John Aston and Jimmy Ryan.

United, of course, had built up a very successful side which won the European Cup, and the great names were Denis Law, Bobby Charlton, George Best and Paddy Crerand. Perhaps, after that triumph of 1968, it would have been best to break up the team, and give some of the younger players their head. Bill Shankly made no bones about breaking up a successful side at Liverpool, and the result was that the Anfield club maintained its record of success without any real transitional period.

I am not suggesting that Matt Busby was at fault. I have written about the manager-player relationship, and it is a difficult one for both parties, at the best of times. The Busby record over the years had stood – and still stands – scrutiny, and for my part, I have the greatest admiration for what United's manager of those days achieved. Matt Busby taught me something, indeed, which shaped my views on life. I had joined the club as an amateur, and made my first-team bow still as an amateur – it was in my first year at university, and my debut was against Stoke City at the Victoria Ground. At the club's request, I signed part-time professional forms in my final year at the University, and once I had gained my degree, the next and obvious step was to make professional football a full-time occupation.

So we started negotiating, and United offered to pay me a wage of £50 a week. I had other ideas, and I asked for £60 a week. It wasn't merely that I had decided I would be like Oliver Twist and ask for more, whatever they had proposed; I genuinely felt that I had a good case for asking for the figure I have mentioned. While I had been at university, and still an amateur footballer, I had been catching the bus to Old Trafford or United's training ground at The Cliff, and putting in a full training session before the professionals reported in a morning, or doing my training between lectures. In short, I had been doing two jobs utterly conscientiously, and I felt that I had given United the sort of dedication which matches that of a real, full-time professional.

Now, when I was being asked to become one, I believed I should reap my reward. I had given the pound of flesh, without complaint, and done as much as a full-timer even though I had been an amateur. And this was the basis of my argument for a wage of £60 a week. I also reflected wryly that during my time at university, I had spent some sleepless nights wondering how the hell I could maintain my double life – giving my studies full attention, while at the same time ensuring that I didn't neglect my Soccer training by even one iota. It reached the stage, indeed, where I was close to a nervous breakdown, because the strain of the physical effort involved, coupled with the mental fatigue which resulted from studying long and hard, had taken toll.

Fortunately, I managed to stay sane, and to get through that demanding period without any distastrous effects. And, of course, when I had played for the first team as an amateur, even though my experience was so limited, I hadn't received, or expected to receive, payment as a professional. But when I raised the question with Matt Busby, he said ' No.'

He was shrewd, he was gentle, and he was his usual urbane self, as he explained his view of the situation. I was a bit upset, and after promising to think over what he had said, I went back to see him again. This time, he said: "Look . . . you show me you can do it, and I'll see that you don't miss out." So, taking him at his word, I accepted what he said. And at the end of the season, I received through the post the offer of a contract which showed that Matt Busby had been every bit as good as his word. I had shown him what I could do, as a professional footballer, and the offer was one which I could not refuse. That little episode showed me that if you put something into your job, you will duly get your reward.

I don't suppose it's everyone who can say that they scored their first goal in League football against the world's greatest 'keeper, but when I look back at my days with United, I'm happy to think I stuck one past Gordon Banks, the day I made my bow at Stoke. The goal came from a corner by George Best, and as the ball came into the centre, Stoke centre-half Denis Smith and a United player challenged for possession, and both of them missed it. The ball dropped for me to volley it home past Banks, and my day was made when we won 4–2.

Around that time, also, I had a problem of loyalty, for I was still playing for England as an amateur, and I had played for the Great Britain Olympic side in a qualifying game against Spain. I was also due to play in an amateur international against Scotland, which meant that I wouldn't be able to follow up my game against Stoke with an Old Trafford debut against Liverpool. But Matt Busby secured my release, and I played in the 1–1 draw against Liverpool.

In the early days, of course, I was a stand-in for a star. I was the man who went into action if Denis Law or Bobby Charlton were injured, and although I wore a number made famous by one or the other, I didn't kid myself that I was another Law or another Charlton. Indeed, I still believed – as I believe now – that my most effective position was in midfield, rather than as an out-

and-out striker, although it's nice to know other people have sufficient faith in you to send you out with the object of scoring goals.

It might be thought that, coming into the professional atmosphere from university life, as I did, there would be some resentment of me by the established professionals who had never known anything but Soccer as an occupation. That wasn't the case, although I had to take some good-natured ribbing about my academic qualifications. I think the other players realised that I'd done my share of grafting at training, during the time I had been studying, and I found that they accepted me easily enough.

Denis Law, for instance, went out of his way on one occasion to make me feel a part of the set-up at the club. We had been to a function, and when it was ending, Denis was going on to a favourite Italian restaurant of his in Manchester for a meal. He invited myself and Lynn, who is now my wife, to join his party, and both of us appreciated the gesture very much.

In one way, I'm a fatalist, believing that what will be will be. In another, I suppose I'm superstitious, because I have a routine which I follow in the dressing-room before every game, and if we go on a winning run, I don't change my suit on match days until the run is broken. Other players, I have found, have their own routine, and one of the most amusing was the routine adopted by Nobby Stiles before a game.

As soon as Nobby entered the dressing-room, he would take off all his clothes and don all his football kit, bar his boots. Then, as if he had received some secret signal, he would take all his kit off again, and go and have a wash, or rinse his face in cold water. Next, he would put his contact lenses in, and finally, he would put on his football kit again. And once we got out on the field, he would always bend down and tie up the laces of his boots once more. It was a ritual he never failed to observe.

My early outings in Manchester United's first team were as the stand-in, as I have said. I would be wearing the jersey normally worn by Denis Law, or Bobby Charlton, or George Best. Naturally, the United supporters were disappointed when they learned that one of their idols was out of the side through injury, and I found that the vociferous minority didn't really take to me. I was no stylist; I had a gangling sort of appearance; and I am not what one of my former managers, Gordon Lee, would call a 'coffee-house ball juggler.' So I took a bit of stick at times from the Stretford-enders.

It meant that my initiation into professional football was a somewhat hard one, but that early lack of appreciation of my style stood me in good stead. And I also realised that if the vociferous minority didn't rate me much, the quieter, more discerning majority seemed to appreciate that I was doing my job as well as I knew how.

I wouldn't have been human, if I hadn't worried about it for a while, but when things like that happen, I tend to adopt a fatalistic approach. And while I might never have become an idol of the fans at Old Trafford, I think that in the end, when I left – and possibly afterwards – most of the United supporters had come to appreciate that if nothing else, they knew I could be relied upon for 90 minutes' honest endeavour . . . and a few goals. One or two of them even told me they would like to see me still there.

The relationship between players and fans is a variable one. The fans pay the wages, and so they are tolerated. Acknowledging this fact, the player tries to keep them happy in his relations with them off the field, as well as by his displays on it, for he is constantly aware that the fans are the people who help to keep him in the football industry.

He is also aware, of course, as I have instanced briefly, that the fans can be critical, cruel and impudent. The players do appreciate what they term the 'real' supporters – those who follow the team all over the country, through good times and bad, without causing trouble – but in general they can be critical of the public ignorance and fickleness of opinions. In the players' eyes, the outside world has no conception of what is involved in being a professional footballer.

The fans judge individual players and a team on the display and the result – especially the result – on a Saturday afternoon. They certainly do not relate their own, five-day-week job to that of the player. And because the fans watch football in THEIR leisure time, they often fail to appreciate that football also is a job that is carried on right through the week. Further, the fans are fickle, and their memories are short.

To give you an instance, I can remember a game at Old Trafford when John Aston – who, remember, became a hero with his display in Manchester United's European Cup-winning side of 1968 – could seemingly do little right, on this particular night. Consequently, he was coming in for some terrible abuse from spectators. Suddenly, however, he got the ball and, for once, it ran truly for him, and he scored an exceptionally good goal. In a flash, those same, critical spectators were on their feet and applauding. Aston had become a hero again.

So people can be cruel to a player having a poor game; they can forget all the good games he may have had. And even in the duration of a game, as I have shown, they can rapidly revise their attitude, one moment cursing a player for his faults, the next singing his praises for having scored a good goal. The fans are not appreciative of mistakes, even though the player may not be wholly to blame – they fail to see, for instance, that a bad pass was given because the ball hit a lump in the pitch at the moment he made the pass.

And the fickleness of fans can destroy a player's confidence, so that he becomes frightened of receiving the ball, in case he doesn't make the best use of it and comes in for another avalanche of abuse.

It cuts both ways, of course. Most players will gladly acknowledge that there is no better situation than to have the crowd cheering the team on. Then, the adrenalin starts to flow, and the players respond to the enthusiasm. There have been many cases where encouragement from the fans has given a team the uplift necessary for it to get back into the game, and even retrieve a cause which looked to be lost.

I said that fans can be impudent, in players' eyes, and this impudence may take the form of approaches in the street or in a pub, with fans making criticisms or comments, asking questions which demand a controversial reply, or even offering advice as if they knew the game inside-out. So often players have to be polite and diplomatic, when in the public eye, though deep down they really feel that they are being subjected to a harangue from someone who doesn't even understand what he is taking about. The onlooker sees most of the game, maybe, but he also often thinks he knows more than the experts. There are a million armchair managers for every one who does occupy the hot seat.

Players are always in demand, especially when the team is doing well. They are invited to attend functions, and blasted if they have to refuse an invitation. When they do attend, the players are conscious that many eyes are upon them, and so they cannot really relax. Most times, a player will bite his tongue when he feels that his privacy is being intruded upon, or that someone is trying to needle him. But now and again, he is provoked into a reaction.

As one player put it, when he was talking about a certain function he had attended: 'A right bloody drag. You try to stick together and chat, but every time you look up, someone is steaming across the room to claim you.'

And another instance, where a player had been buttonholed by someone he didn't know from Adam. 'Came charging over, all very public-school. "Ah say, old chap, gather you come from Manchester, what? – Know it quite well . . . used to live at Wilmslow. And you?" I told him, "Moss Side" . . . you should have seen him sheer off, quick.'

I might seem to be taking too big a swipe at too many people, and I know that it is dangerous to generalise. But facts are facts. And I have, I hope, made it clear that in the main, the players have every respect for what they call the genuine fans – usually the folk who, they feel, are from the same sort of background as themselves, and who really have the best interests of the team at heart.

Basically, I have got on well with the fans at Manchester, Huddersfield and Newcastle. And in the case of the two Uniteds, no one can deny that they have supporters who offer a lot of devotion to the cause of the respective clubs. When Newcastle returned as losers from the League Cup final in 1976, the team received a fantastic reception at St. James's Park. The enthusiasm of the supporters could not have been bettered anywhere.

I think it is fair to say that the players at Newcastle had helped in no small measure to cement a good relationship with the supporters, for we had become particularly conscious of the gap which can exist between the fans and the men they go to watch every Saturday. So we tried hard to let our supporters see that they meant something to us. We attended sports forums, visited hospitals, taking gifts to the younger patients and signing autographs, and we did not begrudge the time we spent on such functions. I am certain that our efforts over the months paid dividends, and that gradually we established a real – and valued – relationship with the Newcastle United supporters.

It isn't sufficient for professional footballers to go out and play for 90 minutes in front of the crowd, then to disperse and give no more thought to the people who have paid their hard-earned money to watch you. There has to be a link, and at Newcastle we have done our best to bridge the gap and provide such a link, because we have a common bond – the success of the team and the club. I believe some measure of the success we have achieved in establishing this link can be seen when we play on other grounds around the country, for there is always a solid core of support for Newcastle, and the players certainly appreciate the cheers they hear from the terraces.

3 A Clash of Personalities

'We'll be the best runners, but we won't be able to bloody play!'

'What d'you want – effing blood?'

'No wonder we can't play on a Saturday . . . our legs are too bloody tired to carry us!'

Typical comments on a particularly gruelling training session. And if the results are going badly, players are not too keen to take all the blame upon their own shoulders. They'll criticise the trainers and coaches, and the manager for his tactics or team selection.

'We see that little bloody ball, and we don't know what it is! The training's boring . . . they're supposed to make it interesting . . . they go away to bloody summer coaching courses for new ideas, but it's always the bloody same, year after year!"

Constant pressure on a player during training can get on his nerves and bring about a swift and open reaction. 'He's always on at me. I can't do anything right, for him. I don't enjoy it any more."

One example of such a clash led to a player being disciplined and sent home for seven days by his manager. The incident happened during the half-time period of a reserve game, and the exchange became so fierce that it almost ended in blows. The player felt he was being singled out all the time in training and during the game, and – of course – he was suffering the constant frustration of almost permanent reserve-team football.

Sometimes, during a game, the spectators can see a heated exchange going on between a player and the touch-line bench, where the backroom men sit. Even if the player cannot hear all the comments from the dug-out, the substitute will probably let him know what was said, after the game.

'He didn't half call Fred for not trying. Said he hadn't tried a bloody leg all the game.'

After the match, the trainer may have forgotten the comments he was making during the heat of the moment, and then he will try to make his points in a much more civilised manner. And there are many times when players and training staff can enjoy mutual relaxation, especially if the team is doing well. And all the time, it is the manager, the man at the head of the organisation (so far as the players are concerned) who has to keep things on an even keel. If he shows the strain is telling, the mood quickly rubs off on the players.

Manchester United, under Matt Busby, had an aura of its own. Busby was the epitome of diplomacy, at all times, and although there were ructions on occasions during my period at Old Trafford, by and large 'the boss' managed to ensure that the dirty linen was washed behind closed doors. He could be firm, but he didn't broadcast the club's problems, or his methods of treatment for the ailments.

However, as time went on, it became inevitable that even Matt Busby, able to take the strain as he was, must vacate the managerial chair. He didn't appear to have been affected by the pressure of just about the most demanding job in the game, and even now, when I meet him once or twice a year, he seems not a day older than the first time I saw him. Yet time moves on, and Manchester United could not have him as their manager for ever, and so the change had to be made.

I felt that the side which had done so well needed to be broken up, that other players who had been less in the limelight were in danger of being stifled, and their ambitions being killed. I think Matt Busby realised that it was a time for change, all round and, this being so, he was prepared to give someone else the job of making a fresh start. He was due a break, no doubt about that. He had earned the right to be able to relax a little.

The choice as Busby's successor fell upon Wilf McGuinness. And for me, he was on a loser from the start. When Bill Shankly departed from Liverpool, the club preserved the continuity by appointing Bob Paisley as team boss, and no doubt Manchester United wanted to ensure that the continuity was preserved, by appointing someone from within the club. But the two situations were different, in that Paisley was considerably older and, therefore, acknowledged as wiser, than the men he was to command.

Wilf McGuinness, although on the backroom staff, was still a contemporary of many of the stars at Old Trafford. He had been their team-mate on many occasions – and, indeed, some of them were still more experienced than him. Or they considered themselves to be.

As a coach, and one who knew the United set-up and style, Wilf was well liked. But it was another thing altogether when he was given what amounted to the job of rebuilding the team. That meant some household names in the game were going to find themselves taking a back seat. It might not happen overnight, but the writing was on the wall. Wilf's own career had had its highlights, but it had been cut short by injury, and some of the players undoubtedly felt that he hadn't the pedigree they had. Yet, as manager, he was going to have to sit in judgement upon them – and, probably, wield the axe.

I cannot comment on Wilf's tact or diplomacy, but I know that before long, there was an atmosphere, because certain players made it clear that they didn't agree with his decisions. It was being said, indeed, that some players eventually were making their feelings plain to Matt Busby on the situation. Apart from the atmosphere and the reaction to Wilf's decisions, there were the problems of personality clashes between players, and George Best was starting to cause problems for the club.

Yet people still expected that Manchester United could carry on winning trophies, and this, naturally, was an extra pressure on Wilf McGuinness. Wilf took United to two Cup semi-finals, but in the light of previous regular successes, that wasn't quite sufficient. I began to realise that Wilf didn't really include me in his plans for the future, but, of course, I also appreciated that he was probably more concerned with the problems presented by the star names. So I took a back seat. In the end, I am convinced, it was player problems that caused the axe to fall on Wilf's head – he couldn't overcome those which arose with the senior players.

It was apparent during the Wilf McGuinness era that Bobby Charlton and George Best didn't get on well together, and this conflict of personalities became even stronger after Busby had taken over the reins again. Bobby was the epitome of the professional footballer; he trained 100 per cent, put 100 per cent into every aspect of the game. Best was much more the instinctive footballer, the man who could turn on the flash of genius, and it was easy to see that these two stars had totally differing attitudes towards the game. Bobby believed that players needed to be totally dedicated; George had a different viewpoint and, in his own fashion, he proved it.

Further problems arose when George went missing from training, and when he didn't turn up in time to get the train for a match at Chelsea. Bobby could neither understand this attitude, nor stomach it. The problems George presented caused a lot of heartache for the club, too, when it came to the publicity aspect – I have already said that Matt Busby preferred to try to solve problems within the club, and keep them away from the glare of the spotlight. But it was an almost impossible job, with George. And, to a certain extent, the players generally felt that George's antics were a bit of a let-down which reflected on them, as well as on the club and the player himself.

There was some tremendous talent at Manchester United, of course, and in his own way, each man was an individual. Bobby Charlton could shoot hard, and passed the ball with great accuracy; Paddy Crerand was also an expert passer of the ball, and he could make space; Denis Law was the fearless goal-poacher supreme; and George Best's genius lay in his feet – it made him, quite simply, the best all-round footballer I have ever seen.

And there were younger players who, perhaps, were not so gifted, but were prepared to put every effort into their game . . . but they wondered if they would ever get a real chance. I think that players such as Carlo Sartori, Don Givens, Francis Burns, Jimmy Rimmer – yes, and John Aston and myself – felt that they lived too much and too long in the shadow of the Old Trafford greats.

The younger players, too, felt annoyed with Best, because he was able to take liberties. He showed he could live a life of his own and still produce world-class performances, and I really believe that George, for his part, felt that there were games in which he carried the side. I'm a team man, and I don't subscribe to the view that one man ever made a team; but I have to admit that George pulled out some match-winning performances for Manchester United, and that, in my early days at Old Trafford, I could see how much he contributed, not just by his sheer genius, but by his readiness to chase back and help out in defence, before getting the ball and bringing it away, and setting up or scoring a goal at the other end of the park.

So there was a whole complex situation, and Wilf McGuinness didn't have an easy ride when he was promoted to be the manager of Manchester United. Even though I realised I didn't fit into his plans, it didn't prevent us having a decent working relationship, and there were times, after the axe had fallen, when Wilf would chat to me for long spells about the events of the recent past. What happened to him had its effect, and I believe that when he finally reverted back to coaching, he was almost a broken man. We would sit and talk, and it was clear to me that he felt very sad that, after he had given so much to Manchester United, it should all have ended that way. It left him a bitter man, for a time.

Later, I met him again, when he was managing in Greece, and he told me then that he had become more philosophical about it, although I doubt if he will ever be able to put the pain of that experience completely behind him. During our conversations when we were together at Old Trafford, he gave me a certain insight into what had happened, so I was able to view the whole matter objectively, having seen both sides of the picture.

In football, you learn to read signs. You also come to realise that there are few people who are totally honest, in the sense that they will walk straight up to you, look you in the eye, and tell you that you're not going to do the job, so far as they're concerned. I found, during Wilf's reign as manager, that I could read the signs, and they didn't point to my emergence as a regular first-teamer. I don't recall playing in the first team, in fact, during Wilf's spell as manager, and I sometimes wondered if he distrusted my university background.

I think there is a general suspicion among the dyed-in-the-wool professionals who see someone coming in from an academic background, and it takes time to become accepted. Yet I knew that, even as an amateur, I had worked as hard as any professional at United when it came to putting in the training – harder, because I'd been doing a demanding job at university, as well. The run-of-the-mill professional has seen football as the be-all and end-all of his life from the moment he joined a club, at the age of 16, and professionals as a race are not academically orientated.

I am not saying they lack intelligence; they can work things out for themselves as well as the most accomplished university don. But they are not used to dealing with people from university, and when they see one suddenly in their midst, they are suspicious, until they get to know he is just like themselves. I remember going into the treatment room one day, and Denis Law was there. It wasn't until I mentioned a certain book I'd been reading that Denis pricked up his ears. Yes, he'd read the same book, and that gave us something in common. Further, each of us realised that there wasn't so much difference between us. Some of our interests might be different, but basically we were both down to earth.

As it happens, I'm an Elton John fan, and not so long ago I went to one of his concerts. He didn't know I was in the audience, but during his show, he mentioned my name several times and said some nice things about me – he is, of course, the chairman of Watford Football Club, and a football fan, as well as a showbusiness personality. After the performance, I went backstage to ask if I might just have a word with him . . . and found myself being invited back to his hotel for coffee and sandwiches. There, we talked football for an hour or more, and it emphasised to me yet again how two people from different backgrounds can get together and enjoy conversation on a mutual plane.

On the whole, I found few problems in my days at Manchester United, so far as having a university background was concerned, and I honestly think that the players there realised I was doing my level best to make a success of the same career they themselves had chosen. I never mentioned how the dual role had almost given me a nervous breakdown, at a time when I was going for part one of my finals, and I felt under such tremendous pressure all the way round.

Some of the players may have had a hard time as youngsters, by which I mean they might have known real poverty; I came from a middle-class family where I never knew what it was to go short – but I had my hard times trying to cope with working hard for exams and, at the same time, putting in as much as the professionals when it came to Soccer.

There were occasions, as I've said, when I would wake up during the middle of the night and my brain would be racing, as I thought: 'How the hell am I going to keep going? Am I trying to do too much, studying for a degree and trying to become a professional footballer at the same time?' It was a phase that passed, but while it lasted, it was very uncomfortable, and made my life a misery, at times.

So, when I talked to Wilf McGuinness about what had happened to him, I was able to appreciate the kind of mental torture he must have suffered while, at the same time, trying to take a balanced view of the overall situation, in so far as it had also affected the players under his command. Once Wilf had reverted to coaching, Matt Busby took charge at the club, and I was back in the first-team reckoning almost immediately. It was inevitable that Matt had to bridge the gap again, for there was no one more experienced than he, and the club obviously needed a breathing space before appointing a manager from outside.

It was during Busby's second spell that George Best missed the game at Chelsea, where I was down as substitute, and this meant I played. We won, 3–2, and I scored one of the goals. It was probably one of the best I shall ever score. The ball was punched out by United's goalkeeper, Alex Stepney, and it dropped at my feet, about 25 yards away from our goal. I turned and ran, knocking the ball over the heads of two Chelsea players, collected it again, and was well into the Chelsea half of the field when Ron Harris came racing across to try to stop me.

I veered to the right-hand side of the penalty area, and hit a shot across Peter Bonetti, who got a hand to the ball, but it bounced over the line before being cleared. After that, I was generally in the side, and I had the satisfaction of scoring four goals in a game against Southampton, and winning the cheers of the United fans at Old Trafford, after what was termed 'a star performance' in front of the home fans, when United beat Tottenham Hotspur 2–1.

That game against the Saints brought a me a hat-trick in eight minutes, and it was the first time a United forward had scored four goals in a League match for four years. Southampton's centre-half, John McGarth, gave me what was termed 'a battering' that day and, at the end, paid me the compliment of saying: 'The lad is certainly brave.'

The return of Matt Busby marked a noticeable change in the atmosphere at the club – the senior players were more relaxed, probably because they felt more secure, and everyone benefited, although we all realised it was merely a matter of time before another man arrived to take charge on a permanent basis. He turned out to be Frank O'Farrell, from Leicester City, and I must confess when I learned of the appointment I felt – like every other professional, I suppose – distinctly apprehensive.

I've mentioned the player-manager relationship earlier, and you never can tell whether you will get the nod of approval or the chopper from a new boss. You hope you'll make the right impression on him . . . you know, for sure, that in his first weeks at the club, he will be casting a critical eye over the place and assessing every player on the staff. Malcolm Musgrove also arrived, as Frank O'Farrell's right-hand man, and the initial impression was that this set-up could be beneficial to the club.

You could sense that there was a fresh wind blowing – the training routine was changed from that of the previous years – and when I played two games up front in the Watney Cup warm-up to the season, I was optimistic that things would go well for me. We lost at Luton and Fulham, however, and it became clear that Frank O'Farrell would be considering ringing the changes. I was one of the players who felt the draught, when he told me he intended to leave me out of the side, when United played a friendly against Coventry City.

I still believed that my best position was in midfield, so – while accepting that I was going to be dropped – I said to Frank: 'If you're going to leave me out, give me a chance to play in midfield in the reserves.'

Frank didn't leave me out – he switched me to midfield for the game against Coventry, and we won that match.

It marked the start of a successful run for me in what I considered to be my best position. I kept my place in the side, and as the League season progressed, Manchester United went top of the First Division, and five points clear of the rest of the field. Everything, is seemed, was coming up roses under the new managerial set-up, while my own career blossomed still further, as I was named skipper of the England Under-23 side which played Switzerland at Portman-road, Ipswich.

That was around the end of November, and the United players went to Jersey for a few days' break. Things never seemed to be the same again, unhappily. We won our next match, against Nottingham Forest, then gave an indifferent display when we lost against Leeds United. Things began to fall apart at the seams, with George Best playing up again, as well. When you're winning, you can paper over many of the cracks that are in the facade, but when the results start going wrong, those cracks begin to appear again, in no uncertain manner. And that was how it was at Manchester United.

I was disappointed, when Frank O'Farrell axed me from the first team, because I didn't think I had been play-ing too badly – no worse, at any rate, than several other players who retained their places. I had contributed to the team effort in a positive way, and I felt that I had suf-fered because I wasn't one of the star names in the side, and that it was easier to drop Gowling than one of the more illustrious personalities. From the Christmas, I was back in the reserves, and I began to read about a possible transfer for me.

The day dawned when conjecture became translated into fact, for I was asked if I would fancy a move to London, and Crystal Palace. I politely but firmly declined that opportunity, preferring to soldier on as I was.

Then I was drafted back into the first team – this time not in a midfield role, but as a striker. It was for an FA Cup-tie at Preston and, as usual, I was prepared to give of my best for 90 minutes, despite the disappointment I had suffered. Although I still believed that I was best suited to a midfield role – the position in which I had captained the England Under-23 side against the Swiss – I have never been one of those players who claims his role in the side is inviolate. When I sign for a club, I accept that the club has the right to play me in any position it requires.

We won the Cup-tie at Deepdale, and I scored both our goals. In the foyer at Deepdale, after the game, Frank O'Farrell went out of his way to thank me for the job I had done up front, and he said words to the effect that it was people like myself who deserved to get a lot more out of the game. I thought that perhaps my star was rising once more, but I was wrong.

We went on a close-season tour of Israel, Greece and Majorca, and by the time I returned from foreign parts, I had read the signals all over again . . . I knew deep down, without a shadow of doubt, that I was out in the cold. Right through the tour, I had been stripped and changed into playing kit, ready for the action . . . but each time my role had turned out to be a passive one, for I never got closer than being named as substitute.

Shortly after our return, the telephone rang, and the message was that I was required to go and see Frank O'Farrell. When we met, face to face, he told me that Huddersfield Town had put in an offer for me, and I felt so depressed and disillusioned that I immediately agreed to talk to Ian Greaves, Town's manager at the time. I recalled how I had missed an England Under-23 game against Wales, to ensure that I recovered from injury to play for United; how other happenings had affected my career.

For instance, at the time things began to go badly for United, I was hoping to play for the Under-23 side against Scotland at Derby, and so further my international ambitions. But one day Frank O'Farrell pulled me to one side during training and told me that when the England team manager, Sir Alf Ramsey, had phoned him to check on me, the United boss had told him I was having a bad time, and that he shouldn't bother picking me. Maybe Frank thought he was being absolutely honest, and that his attitude should command my respect. But from that moment, so far as I was concerned, I knew that whatever had gone before, our relationship from then on was soured. There was no way he and I were going to establish any kind of real rapport.

At the end of the season, I had told Frank I thought certain players were getting away with murder, and that I and some of the other young players were being the scapegoats. I felt Frank had been a little bit too quick to sum up the situation, especially with regard to myself, for it was only my second season as a full-time professional. I believed I had something to offer Manchester United, but it seemed that Frank didn't agree.

And so, when he called me in and told me that Huddersfield wanted to sign me, these memories came flooding back, and I was sick at heart . . . so I didn't hesitate, as I told him I would speak to Ian Greaves. And you have my word for it that when I signed for Town, I really signed for the man. It was one of the major mistakes of my life, and one I would never repeat. Not because I misjudged the man, but because I realised later that you can pay a high price for loyalty, and before the end, both Ian and I had suffered.

4 A Transfer — or I Quit

'What did he say?'

'Who?'

'The Chairman.'

'Sorry, I wasn't listening. The usual "Good luck, lads", I suppose. It's always the same. Smug buggers, aren't they? There they are, sipping gin and tonic while some nutcase of a full-back kicking six bags of shit out of us on the pitch."

'They're not all like that.'

'Maybe not. But none of them knows anything about the game. Why don't they leave it all to the boss? He's the pro.'

That may not seem an enervating sort of conversation, but it sums up another relationship in football. The one between directors and players. Very few directors have played the game at professional level. They attain their position on the board by acquiring shares through wealth, or from the family, graduating from the terraces and stands to the directors' box.

Having got there, they will rarely be removed, except by death or by some move from a rival group of businessmen who feel they can run the club in a better, more successful manner.

Few directors are young men. There are the odd exceptions who have received shares from their father at an early age, but on the whole, most directors are over 45.

This is largely because they are successful businessmen, and to achieve that status takes time and hard work in the early years. It is the directors who, in the hard times, will dip their hands into their pockets and put money into the club, and give financial guarantees. It is the directors who, like the manager, the players and the supporters, long and hunger for the sweet taste of success.

In spite of, and because of, the position of the directors, the players have very little interest in them. When I was at Manchester United, I occasionally came into contact with the chairman, Louis Edwards, and other directors, and they seemed pleasant enough individuals. After I joined Huddersfield Town, I came into much closer contact with the chairman, because I was involved in discussions with him about my own career. But that was in the latter days, as I shall relate shortly.

Generally speaking, there is not much affinity between the two groups – players and directors – and maybe it is the natural order of things that it should be this way. Players are not openly rude to directors, and will acknowledge their presence or pass the time of day with them. They do this obviously out of politeness, and more so because their jobs depend, to a certain extent, upon the decisions of directors. Behind the directors' backs, however, players are liable to criticise and ridicule. For they see directors as having little or no knowledge of the game. Certainly not as they themselves see it.

Because directors, generally speaking, have never played the game professionally (Sir Matt Busby, Len Shackleton, Alec Stock and a handful of others have known professional involvement), players question their right to comment, and even to direct the fortunes of a club. 'It's easy for the directors to talk and criticise – they've never played the bloody game.'

Players enjoy poking fun at or aping people in every walk of life, but the directors are often the peculiar target. If a director has a word to say to the players, or appears nearby, there is almost inevitably some comment or mickey-taking, once he has gone. It is true to say that there are directors who command the respect of players, so, as in everything else, there are exceptions to the rule.

On the whole, however, there is a big gap between the two groups. This may be a relic of tradition, when in the old days there was much more a master-servant relationship, and there is also the age difference. The players rarely see the directors together as a unit, except at a Christmas party or on a tour abroad. The policies of the directors are seldom explained to the players and, because they are thus ignorant of the reasoning behind a decision which may seriously affect them, players are quick (perhaps over-quick) to criticise.

In the players' eyes, the times they see the directors are the times when the directors themselves are relaxing. In this respect, when the directors are seen to be consistently drinking – in the bar before a pre-match meal, wine with the meal, then drinks at half-time and after the game. There are times when the players are sitting waiting on the coach after a game for the directors to finish their social chat and their drinks. Drinking may be a directorial habit and, indeed, players can knock back the booze. But they are especially critical of directors who appear to be in a constant state of intoxication.

What happens on occasions when directors are 'well oiled' is that they can become loose-tongued, and will say things to players which are not necessarily conducive to improving the atmosphere in a club. At the same time they lay themselves open to criticism, and embarrass players.

In the dressing-room before a game, often the chairman

is the only director allowed to come in and wish the players good luck. Even in this case, the atmosphere created by the players is one of indifference. Kick-off time is looming, and players are too concerned, on the whole, with their pre-match routine to pay much attention to what the chairman says. They consider often enough that it's only a platitude, anyway.

The players, nevertheless, must accept some responsibility for the situation. The blame is not one-sided. Players do isolate themselves from directors, whether consciously or not. They see their interests and the interests of the directors as being separate, and they also see themselves as being subordinate to the directors and, therefore, subject to the directors' will. To attempt to mix too freely with the directors is to invite criticism from team-mates of 'creeping' and 'arsehole-licking.' Players are very conscious of other players' criticism, and seek their approval and support. In their opinion, it is the players who know each other's problems. According to the players, directors are on a different wavelength, because of wealth or age.

When the team is travelling, the two groups maintain their isolation. The players want to be with their own kind – one of the lads, and nothing more. They play cards and chat, in almost total oblivion of the presence of directors. On tour, perhaps, the two groups get closer, for the pressures are relaxed; they are experiencing the same events and places, and have a common relationship which is less restrictive.

In trying to present a balanced view of the relationship, it must also be remembered that directors have similar feelings as players do – about wanting success for the club, about winning matches, about referees. For, like the players, directors experience rivalries with other clubs. And they often have the same opinions of the fans as do the players. Yet this still does not create a greater under-standing between the groups. And once the club tour is over, the curtain falls back into place. The tour, and the directors, may be brought up by the players later, but as a source of complaint or amusement, and not as a foun-dation of friendship. Frankly, I believe there is a crying need for greater communication between the boardroom and players, in football generally. Only in that way will players and directors achieve a greater understanding of each other's problems, even though the problems may be different.

When I left Manchester United for Huddersfield Town, I was travelling in a downward direction. I say this with no feeling of bitterness, because I went into it with my eyes wide open. Ironically, Manchester United, once one of Soccer's poor relations, were a club which had risen to the pinnacle; while Huddersfield, once one of Soccer's giants, had slipped down the scale. Huddersfield had had their problems with players before I arrived, because they and some of their stars – Frank Worthington, Trevor Cherry and Roy Ellam – had not seen eye to eye on some issues. That was no concern of mine. I was going to cost Huddersfield £65,000, but before I signed, I wanted to weigh up the whole situation for myself, in spite of my disillusion with the way events had turned out for me at Old Trafford.

Town had been relegated to the Second Division, and they were obviously intent on making their way back to the top flight as quickly as possible. When I saw their manager, Ian Greaves, I was impressed immediately: not only with the ambitions he expressed, but also by his total honesty; for he made it clear that, while I might con-sider myself a midfield man, he wanted me to play up front, in a striking role. In return, I said I would play any-where he wanted, if I decided to sign for Huddersfield.

Ian expounded on his aims, and I became more and more impressed by his directness. I felt that here was a man who knew what he wanted, and that I could work closely with him to help achieve the objective. He wanted me to take on considerable responsibility, for apart from scoring goals, he thought I could help in the development of the younger players.

We seemed to strike up a tremendous relationship from the start – although, in retrospect, I would never allow myself to get as close to a manager again. For in the later days at Huddersfield, the fact that I was so close to him rebounded on me. And that made for the unhappiest period of my life as a professional footballer.

The bald fact is that Huddersfield, instead of climbing straight back to the First Division, slid down to the Third. I had scored 17 goals during our season in the Second Division, and I scored 25 goals the season we were in the Third Division, so I think I can claim that I fulfilled the role Ian had wanted me to play. He knew, when we suffered relegation, that I wasn't happy at the prospect of playing in Third Division football, but when we discussed the matter, he persuaded me to give it one more go, and see if we couldn't bounce straight back.

That was in the close season, just after we had dropped out of the Second Division. I agreed to his proposal, went away on holiday, returned home, and was cutting the lawn when a neighbour came across to tell me the news. Ian had resigned as manager of Huddersfield. There had been a shake-up at boardroom level, and I discovered shortly afterwards that I was required to go and see the new chairman, Stanley Kinder. I explained the situation to him, as I had explained it to Ian, and finally I agreed that I would stay and help the club to try to get out of the Third Division. We reached a gentleman's agreement that if things didn't improve, I would then be allowed to leave.

Bobby Collins, who had been a star with Everton and Leeds United, was appointed team manager, and we set out to try to gain promotion. As it turned out, the season went badly for the club, and instead of a place in the Second Division, it became obvious that we were going to have a struggle to stear clear of the Fourth. Bobby was a professional, all right – sometimes I felt that he was too much of one, and there were times when our ideas didn't match. We had one or two verbal sparring sessions when we were out training, although I think that deep down, we could each understand and have a healthy respect for one another. Bobby had been through the mill, too, and in this, his first managerial job, it was hard going.

The arrival of Tom Johnston from York, as general manager, meant a change in the status of Bobby Collins, for it soon became clear that Tom was the 'gaffer'. I went to see Tom, and explained about the gentleman's agreement I had with the chairman. He knew nothing about this, he said, so together we went to see Mr. Kinder, who acknowledged that there was, in fact, such an agreement. However, both men did their best to persuade me to forget it.

It wasn't as simple as that for me, however, and I made it plain that I would like to leave the club, under the gentleman's agreement we had made.I was conscious, of course, that Huddersfield had me under contract – I had signed for four years, with a four-year option, when joining forces with Ian Greaves. That's what I meant when I talked about having signed for the man. Now, in my view, the situation had been completely transformed, for in the space of time that I had been at Huddersfield, I was serving under my third manager.

Privately, I acknowledged to myself that had I been in the shoes of the chairman or Tom Johnston, I would have done the same as they did, and tried to persuade the player to stay. When it was clear that I remained unmoved, however, it was agreed – reluctantly by them – that I would be allowed to move, although I would have to appreciate that this might not be possible overnight. In short, I would have to be prepared to accept a period of waiting.

Time kept going on, and I kept receiving the same answer – that other clubs had not been showing an interest in me – and the transfer deadline came and went, without a move for me. Things were going from bad to worse for the club, on the field, and we heading for the Fourth Division. Apart from that, the economics of the situation were becoming more and more apparent, for we had to cut down on expenses all the way round.

Overnight stays were eliminated, whenever possible, and when we did stay at a hotel, it wasn't top grade any longer. I remember on one occasion when we did stay overnight, I roomed with Rod Belfitt, and as he tried to open the wardrobe, the whole piece of furniture almost collapsed. The curtains at the bedroom window were a long way from being wide enough to meet, when you drew them, so it was a question of deciding whether to have the space at each side or in the middle. We finally agreed to draw the curtains together, and have the morning light coming in at each side of the window.

There was a draught coming from the window, as well, and we could do nothing about that. The bedclothes were not long enough to cover me, either, so I finished up lying there shivering, with the clothes covering me from the waist down, and a towel draped around my shoulders. Then I got up and put my overcoat on the top half of the bed, to try to keep warm. It wasn't the ideal preparation for a match the following day, although in the end, we had to laugh.

At the end of the season, Huddersfield Town suffered the indignity of being relegated once again, and so they were in the Fourth Division. Mr. Kinder relinquished the chairmanship, and I went on holiday to do a lot of hard thinking. I came to the conclusion that if, as had been said on more than one occasion, there really was no one interested in me, then I might as well turn my back on professional football and try to make a living in business.

I still believed that I had something to offer to a club in a higher division, still felt that if I were going to be reduced to Fourth Division football, after having played for England Under-23 and in the First Division with Manchester United, I might as well decide this was the end of the road. I had started my footballing career with Stockport Schoolboys, playing at Edgeley Park, the home of Stockport County, and I had made a vow to myself that I would never return to Edgeley as a Fourth Division player. It was a personal standard I had set for myself.

Moving from Manchester United to Second Division football with Huddersfield had not been too bad, especially as I had been influenced by my impressions of Ian Greaves, the man for whom I had signed. My relationship with Ian kept me at Huddersfield when further misfortune befell the club, and I had agreed to Ian's request to give it a go, when the club had dropped into Division 3. But then Ian had gone, and I had only my own career to think about. Now, I was absolutely determined that, come what may, I would not descend to the Fourth Division and complete obscurity.

I was facing facts, and I had come to a decision. But I don't think Tom Johnston and the new chairman really appreciated that I meant what I said. I don't think they realised I was in deadly earnest.

When I went to see the chairman, he offered me no

hope of a move, and the start of the new season brought new problems. By then, I had failed to put in an appearance for pre-season training – a fact which was kept a closely-guarded secret by the club. After I had been conspicuous by my absence for the first couple of days, I received a phone call from Tom Johnston, and he requested my presence at the club, as Crystal Palace – yes, that name cropped up again – were showing interest in me. So I agreed, and went in for training . . . but the week passed by, and no one said anything more to me about Crystal Palace.

Off I went, to try to nail Tom Johnston, and he told me that the deal was virtually set up. He was just waiting for a phone call of confirmation. So I told him that when the phone call did come, I would be obliged if he would ring me at once, at my home. For one reason or another the expected call about Crystal Palace never did materialise, and so that deal fell through. But now Huddersfield could not fail to appreciate my mood of single-minded determination. It was a transfer – or I would quit the game.

The next thing that happened was that I learned a deal had been set up with West Bromwich Albion, who had recently appointed former Leeds player Johnny Giles as their team boss. So I travelled to the Midlands for talks with Johnny, and I must say that I was impressed by his ideas, and his ambitions for promotion from the Second Division. It was no fault of Johnny's that I didn't become a West Brom player. But I did gain the impression from other people at the club that West Brom would be doing me a favour, giving me the chance to climb from Fourth Division football to Second Division Soccer, and the attitude in some quarters there seemed to be: 'You can take it or leave it.'

I wasn't prepared to take it – or leave it – on the spur

of the moment, so I travelled home to give the matter some serious thought. I arrived home about 11.15 that night, and when my telephone rang, it was Tom Johnston at the other end of the line, this time to ask me if I had signed for West Brom. And when I answered that I hadn't, and was giving the whole thing considerably more thought, he surprised me by saying that Gordon Lee, who had recently taken charge as the manager of Newcastle United, had been in touch with Huddersfield about the possibilities of signing me. It was a turn-up for the book, but I immediately agreed to meet Gordon Lee and talk to him, while reserving the right to leave West Brom waiting for my final answer.

I thought back to the time I had left Old Trafford and joined Huddersfield. There had always seemed to be a distance between manager and players at Manchester United, and yet Ian Greaves and I had established an immediate rapport at Huddersfield. I did hear later that one or two of the Town players resented this close liaison between myself and Ian, but nothing was ever said to me about it. I had been saddened by Ian's departure, but as I thought about our relationship, I realised that it would have been better if we had maintained the arm's-length attitude which had existed at Old Trafford. That way, you couldn't get too close to someone, and you didn't risk being hurt or have the feeling of let-down.

When Ian had left Huddersfield, things had turned sour for me, as well as for the club, although I have to say now that even if Ian had stayed, I wouldn't have remained there once the club had dropped into the Fourth Division. Things hadn't been perfect during Ian's reign, partly because the incident concerning Frank Worthington, Trevor Cherry and Roy Ellam had left its mark, with players who had been their team-mates clearly affected by it all.

The descent to Division 4 had meant a tightening of the purse strings, and Bobby Collins had been followed by Tom Johnston. We had had great hopes when Bobby arrived, but the whole thing just fell flat in the end. Tom was a dour character, and I don't think we ever really understood each other. With Bobby, even though we engaged in verbal sparring from time to time, I could appreciate that he knew what he wanted, and I liked his ideas about training; with Tom, I felt we were never on the same wavelength, and that I could not reach a real understanding with him.

Tom had arrived at Huddersfield when the situation was already becoming very difficult, and perhaps really he was being asked to work a miracle. But he was difficult to get to know, and very close. He did things in his own way, and you could never claim to know what he was thinking – when he sat himself down and puffed away at his pipe, the lads used to joke that you needed to be able to read the smoke signals, to find out what was going on in Tom's mind.

For myself, as for the club, the last six months had been tinged with desperation, and I had been faced with the prospect of staying at Huddersfield another five years . . . or getting out. Now, I had the choice of moving up to the Second Division with West Brom, or back to the First Division with Newcastle United – providing Gordon Lee and I saw eye to eye on the things that really mattered. And I'm not talking merely about money.

So I spent a sleepless night trying to weigh up all the possiblities, and finally I decided to let the next day take care of itself. It would be time enough to decide which way I was going, once I had spoken to the Newcastle manager. And it was a satisfying thought that someone still believed I could measure up to the demands at top level.

5 The Deep End Again

Someone once said that Gordon Lee had 'the lean and hungry look.' He has certainly admitted his hunger for success. 'I'm greedy,' he once said. 'I want to go to Wembley, and every year that comes along, I see it as my year. Football is competitive; it's big business – and the prize, for me, is the First Division championship. It's the best division in the world.' It was Gordon who gave me the chance to play again in that 'best division in the world', and to go to Wembley.

He is like Matt Busby, in that he hails from a mining community. I think that Gordon had it rather harder than I did, when he was a youngster, because his father was a miner, and Gordon was the youngest of 10 children. He's come a long way since those days in the Staffordshire village of Hednesford, but he's never forgotten his early upbringing – including the time his Dad caught him smoking, and took off his belt to young Gordon, who was only 13.

I think that Gordon felt at home among the Geordies, even though his accent has the nasal twang of the Midlands, and not the North-East. He once said: ' A lot of people can see problems, but don't do anything to solve them. That's not my way, whether you like it or not. As a manager, I'll make mistakes – who doesn't? – but you only become top in your profession by profiting out of mistakes and being prepared to make them. It has to be my way, and that's that.'

Gordon's rise to prominence as a manager had been some-what meteoric. He was a former player who took charge at Port Vale, then became the man in charge of team affairs at Blackburn Rovers. At that stage of his career he was one of the comparative unknowns on the backroom side of the game. Lean, and with an intense and sometimes brooding look, he got down to the job, generating enthusiasm, and transmitting it to his players. He showed that he is what is known as a good motivator, and his success became apparent when he steered Blackburn Rovers into the Second Division.

The fact that he had taken the Rovers so swiftly to promotion did not escape attention, and it was then that Newcastle United appeared on the scene. The sequal to his departure from Ewood Park to St James's Park was a lengthy and, at times, vitriolic exchange of words be-tween officials of the respective clubs, for Blackburn did not take kindly to Gordon's move to Newcastle. Indeed, the Rovers were so incensed at having lost him that they complained bitterly, and eventually the Football League agreed to investigate the charges of the Rovers' board that there had been unfair dealings by Newcastle. That, now, is all in the past, of course, for Gordon has moved on again, to Everton.

I arranged to meet Gordon Lee for afternoon tea at an hotel at Scotch Corner. I had talked to him in passing when I was at Huddersfield and he, as the manager of Black-burn Rovers, had gone across to sign Bobby Hoy. The prospect of moving from Huddersfield to the North-East did not unduly bother me, since I had friends in the area and had visited them regularly over the previous six years or so. But it still remained to be seen what impression Gordon Lee and I gained of each other, and whether, at the end of the day, he still wanted me, and I wished to join Newcastle United.

I know him a lot better now, but even on that initial meeting, he came across as a man who generated tremendous enthusiasm. He had been manager of Newcastle United only a few weeks, and he was full of plans to ensure that the club made real progress. They had the support, they had the nucleus of a fine side, and they could become one of the top sides in the First Division again, and in Europe. That was Gordon's theme, as we talked about my proposed £70,000 transfer. So I was impressed (shades of Ian Greaves!), but even so, I was a little bit sceptical about his ideas for me; because he wanted me to do a job scoring goals, and I knew that Newcastle United had had Malcolm Macdonald and John Tudor as a striking partnership, and that it had been pretty successful. John was injured at that time, and Gordon's idea was that I would become the striking partner with Malcolm.

I took it with a pinch of salt, because I could visualise a situation where, when John Tudor regained fitness, there would be three men fighting for two places – and, as 'Supermac' must be an automatic choice, that would leave Tudor and myself fighting for the odd spot, with John, through his experience with Malcolm already, bound to have the edge. In the end, however, I decided I had nothing to lose, except the belief that I could still measure up to the demands of top-flight football. I'd wanted the chance to prove myself again – and here it was.

West Brom's offer of a contract was on a take-it-or-leave it basis; Newcastle's offer was a gamble, too. But it was First Division against Second Division, and if I failed, then I would at least know the worst, even if I were being flung in at the deep end again, as had happened when I broke through to the first team with Manchester United. I was that bit older, that bit wiser, and considerably more experienced. And I had learned something from my days in the Second and Third Divisions.

So I told West Brom I would have to decline their offer, with thanks, and signed for Newcastle. I moved in with friends in the area, and when I reported for pre-season training, I found it was the easiest I had ever known. I was pleasantly surprised, but somewhat dubious that it would form a basis for fitness right through the gruelling slog of 42 League matches, in all weathers and under all kinds of conditions. You did some running and some exercises, but Gordon Lee made just about everything a team event. Whether it was tunnel-ball or hand-passing, it was a team effort, and it soon became clear to me that Gordon's idea, first and foremost, was to encourage team spirit. Everyone was expected to pull together. It was all so different from what I had experienced in pre-season training before.

And as the season advanced, I discovered, also, that far from needing to worry about fitness, the players were able to keep right on going, without undue strain. Because you had been working in teams, with the edge of real competition, you had put in every ounce of effort – more, possibly, than you would have done as an individual during a routine training exercise.

Richard Dinnis was also a newcomer to Newcastle United – he had been brought by Gordon from Blackburn – but for the first the season, he was usually on the sidelines, so to speak, assimilating things, while Gordon was in the thick of it all, track-suited and putting the players through their paces. There were times when I suspected that Richard didn't feel he was earning his money, but after that first season, he had given his head, and he showed quickly enough that he knew what was what. Maybe Gordon felt, that first season, that he needed to get to know the players inside-out, and this was his priority. Once Richard became fully involved, it was clear to me that he and Gordon made a good team of their own.

Gordon quickly made an impression – a strong impression – upon me that he was a manager who not only knew his own mind, but was prepared to say his piece in front of anyone, provided he was convinced he was right. The Malcolm Macdonald business certainly gave clear evidence that Gordon was strong enough to stand on his own two feet, and that he was ready to accept the responsibility of running team affairs his own way.

Newcastle United, founded as Newcastle East End in 1892, had an illustrious history. Four times they had finished as First Division champions, and they had won the FA Cup half a dozen times. But perhaps the honours list tells a story in itself, for while Newcastle went to Wembley three times in the 1950's, and carried off the FA Cup on each occasion, while they also won the Fairs Cup in Europe in 1969, the last time they had captured the championship of the First Division had been away back in 1927.

Gordon Lee's views on what real success meant began to colour the atmosphere at St James's Park. He believed that Cups were tin-pot trophies – his idea of success was carrying off the championship of the Football League. And he also made it clear that he had no time for the glamour-boys of the game – he wanted a team of 11 men without stars. That way, he believed, would real success be achieved.

Gordon showed that he was prepared to ring the changes at Newcastle, and he did so, buying players as well as selling. Apart from the eventual transfer of Malcolm

Macdonald, he sold another long-standing favourite, Terry Hibbitt, and Pat Howard and John Tudor moved on. Gordon's attitude was that 'there comes a time when it's good for both players and the club to introduce new faces . . . we had a situation, for instance, with Hibbitt and (Tommy) Craig when it was impossible for both to play on the same team. Both were natural, left-sided players; Hibbitt had established himself and reached a standard which didn't leave much to work on or develop. I felt there was a better future for Craig, so Hibbitt went.'

The manner of Terry's departure will not easily be forgotten by players who were there – mention Terry, indeed, and someone will start talking about a clean shirt. We played in a mid-week match at Derby, and lost, 3–2. Straight after that match, Gordon took Terry on one side (we knew nothing about this, there and then), and the next thing, as we're on the coach and waiting to leave for home, Terry climbed aboard, grabbed his case, and said: 'Good-bye, lads.' Then he told his startled listeners that he was off to sign for Birmingham. So the in-joke became: 'Remember to pack a clean shirt . . . just in case you find you're on your way, after a match!'

I didn't play in the first game after my arrival at St James's Park. That match was virtually a warm-up, against Carlisle in the Anglo-Scottish tournament. Newcastle lost that one, and I was in for the match against Middlesbrough . . . distinguishing myself by scoring an own-goal in a 1–1 draw. Then I played against Sunderland, but we didn't qualify for the next stage of the competition. And so we reached the start of the League season proper, with a difficult first fixture, away against Ipswich Town. Some eyebrows were raised, that Saturday evening, when the results were broadcast, for Malcolm Macdonald scored two goals, I had one disallowed, and we won, 3–0.

After half a dozen matches, Malcolm Macdonald had scored eight goals . . . and I hadn't broken my duck. But I wasn't unduly worried, because I had gone through similar periods before, and I felt that I was playing a full part in the team effort, although I realised well enough that my initial lean spell as a marksman had put a question mark against me, in the eyes of the supporters and the critics. There was nothing I could do, however, except continue to give of my best and hope that I could get among the goals. I did exactly that, when Newcastle played Southport in the League Cup at St James's Park.

Malcolm Macdonald was injured at the time, so this meant that Paul Cannell was his stand-in, and Paul and I forged the twin spearhead for Newcastle. Between us, we rattled in half a dozen goals, and my haul was four of them. From then on, everything seemed to swing round in my favour, and the goals began to flow for me. I still realised that I would never become an idol of the fans like 'Supermac', but that didn't worry me, because I've never had ambitions to hog the headlines. Yet the very fact that I was playing alongside a goal-scoring machine who was the darling of the supporters meant that I had to show I could contribute my share, and so this was an extra kind of pressure, so far as I was concerned.

There was an occasion, in fact, when Gordon Lee shouldered me with a burden for which I certainly hadn't asked. Maybe he thought hard and long before he said his piece, or maybe it was something he said straight off the cuff. Fortunately for both of us, his forecast proved to be accurate, when he said I would finish up by scoring more goals in a season than 'Supermac'. That was in the season Newcastle went to Wembley for the final of the League Cup, and not long afterwards Malcolm moved on to Arsenal. Between these two events, there were rumbles and rumours about the relations between Malcolm and the manager, and about Mal's probable transfer.

The storm that broke upon Gordon Lee's departure from Blackburn was one thing; the storm that broke when there was talk of Malcolm leaving Newcastle was another. There were some players who felt that Malcolm was being pushed out, other who claimed that it was time for him to go. And it was during a club tour of Majorca that the feelings of people inside the Newcastle camp became known.

We used to go down to a bar where we could have a quiet drink and a hamburger, and it was in those surroundings that the Malcolm Macdonald issue was brought into the open. When you've had a drink or two, and you are with people in the game, the talk, naturally, is about football and football people, and tongues become loosened a little. So players who hitherto had kept their thoughts mainly to themselves began to open up, and there were some lively – indeed, heated – discussions about Newcastle United and the future of the club.

Malcolm was on the tour, and the arguments for and against him waxed loud and long. No one disliked him as a person – it was very much a discussion on how much he meant to Newcastle United, how much he contributed to the team effort, whether the goals he scored were worth as much as some people obviously thought they were. And, of course, there was argument, also, about Mal's popularity with the supporters, who had been brought up on Albert Stubbins and Jackie Milburn, and who loved the excitement that Malcolm brought into their lives on a Saturday afternoon. I'm certain that today, although he is now totally involved with the management of Everton, one thing for which Gordon Lee will still vividly remember Newcastle United was the players and the talk on that

The one that got away against West Bromwich Albion.

Another goal against the Spurs.

Anxious moments for the Queen's Park Rangers defence.

Goal! — and Alan Gowling gets a salute from a Newcastle team-mate.

Having just scored against Queen's Park Rangers in the League Cup.

Best foot forward . . . and Alan Gowling rifles home a goal in the F.A. Cup replay against Coventry City.

Above left: Derby games come and go. As a Manchester United player, Alan Gowling knew the excitement of local rivalry against Manchester City. Now the team and the location have changed . . . it's Gowling of Newcastle United . . . and the opposition is . . . still Manchester City.

Below left: Going up for the Cup . . . the League Cup. And it's a Gowling goal that helps to pave the way in a semi-final against Spurs.

Above: Alan Gowling leaves Queen's Park Rangers defender David Webb looking up, as if to say: ' Now what's he going to do?'

Newcastle United and Manchester City were the League Cup finalists of 1976, and here Alan Gowling is pictured in action against City.

Here's another derby game, this time against Newcastle's neighbours and rivals, Middlesbrough. And Alan Gowling fends off a challenge from the Boro' right-back to tuck away a scoring chance for Newcastle.

Airborne . . . Alan Gowling gets up to beat a Birmingham defender.

Two's company, five's a crowd . . . but in this game against Ipswich at Portman-road, Alan Gowling wins the battle for possession in the air, and heads the ball past Kevin Beattie, wearing No. 6 for Ipswich.

Well, we've made it! Team-mate Tommy Craig looks as if he still cannot believe that Newcastle United are through to the League Cup final, but the smile from Alan Gowling confirms it.

Wembley, 1976, and it's Newcastle United v. Manchester City in the final of the League Cup. City 'keeper Joe Corrigan, and defenders Willie Donachie and Tommy Booth watch in despair, Alan Gowling holds his breath . . . but this effort just shaved the wrong side of the City post.

Safe in my arms! And this is one time Alan Gowling is foiled, as the Tottenham 'keeper goes down and gets to the ball first.

No mistake about this one — and scorer Alan Gowling receives the congratulations of a team-mate, as Manchester City players betray their feelings. For them, it's a moment of agony.

No holding back — and it's Ipswich skipper Mick Mills in a tussle for possession with Alan Gowling.

Winning by a head . . . Alan Gowling manages to get to the ball first — and
s' a goal against Everton.

Would you believe it! Alan Gowling's expression says it all, as he sees the ball go just past a post.

Hey, mind me! Alan Gowling and Queen's Park Rangers defender David Webb get into a tangle.

The winners take the trophy, and for the gallant losers, it's a tankard apiece. Manchester City have the League Cup, and here the Newcastle players step up to receive their presentation mementoes. Alan Gowling and Tommy Craig show the disappointment of defeat, after a valiant fight.

close-season tour of Majorca. For people spoke their minds.

Almost from the day we arrived on the island, there were heated arguments between the players, and Gordon and Richard Dinnis joined in the discussions. And, of course, views varied. In any club, you get players who think that professional football is a ten-till-noon job, so far as training goes, and a 90-minute, all-out stint on a Saturday. You get other players who feel deeply that the job demands much more than a cursory attention to it during the recognised hours of attendance at the club. You will also have opposing views about teamwork and star players, and I think it is fair to say that Malcolm, in the eyes of some of his team-mates, placed the emphasis upon the individual, rather than on the team.

There were players whose friendship with him made them feel they must come down on his side; others who felt they could do no more than stay on the fence; and still others who believed that the time had come for them to challenge the 'star' image. Some players felt that for too long they – or the rest of the team – had been living in Malcolm Macdonald's shadow. Up to that tour, perhaps this last group had felt that they were comparatively young and didn't have the experience to speak out . . . but, as I said, alcohol tends to loosen tongues and gives people the courage to speak their minds.

Some of the players felt that Gordon Lee was not strong enough in his position as manager, because we had heard that his head had been on the chopping block on two occasions since he had arrived at the club. The events concerned were a League Cup-tie against Notts. County, and a League match against Burnley. Each time, we won by the only goal of the game. I don't know if Gordon ever knew about the rumours that defeat in either of

c

those matches would have put his job in peril, but certainly the players were in no doubt that, from the early days of his accession to the throne at St. James's, Gordon was under a great deal of pressure, one way and another.

There were certain people who, it appeared, did not take kindly to Gordon's way of running the show – and I'm not referring here to Malcolm Macdonald. There was no doubt that Gordon could show an abrasiveness in his dealings with people. I could only assume that he was as direct in his boardroom manner as in everything else, and it was obvious that there was no love lost between himself and some of the people higher up.

His position had been complicated by the fact that quite a lengthy time elapsed while he was living in an hotel, which meant a separation from his family, and he did not sign his contract until we had won the semi-final of the League Cup in 1976, and were at Wembley. We felt that between our semi-final victory and our appearance at Wembley, Gordon was in as strong a position as he ever would be and, in retrospect, I think that he would probably agree with this view. Then was the time to nail things down, and get it established that he had full powers, so far as the playing side was concerned.

By the time that we had been to Wembley and lost the League Cup final against Manchester City, it meant, in our view, that he had to be at least as successful the following season, to stand any chance of having a similar opportunity to gain real power. He is a patient man, and I think he really believed, then, that in his own way, and in his own time, he would be able to change things. I think he also believed that he would be able to convert other people to his way of thinking. It was only in the latter days that he came to realise there was no way he could win.

While we were in Majorca, Gordon intimated that

Malcolm Macdonald didn't fit into his plans. Basically, we doubted that Gordon would get his own way on this aspect of the situation – our view was that seeing was believing. To see him sell Malcolm was to believe . . . and, finally, it did happen. We were then convinced as to Gordon's strength, both as regards Malcolm and the board.

There had been one occasion, in fact, when the players were disappointed in Gordon, and that was after a game against Leeds, in which Malcolm had been given the job of marking Duncan McKenzie at corner kicks. McKenzie had scored a goal with a header from a corner, and at the team meeting afterwards, Mal just wouldn't admit that he had made a mistake. When Gordon didn't push the issue, we felt a bit let down.

There was another time when we had beaten Coventry City 4–0 at St James's Park – Malcolm and I had gone eight matches without getting a goal, and in that game the goals came from a full-back and a midfield player. The Sunday papers were full of the fact that Malcolm was unhappy with his new role of playing more deeply and making goals, and helping to create goals for me. This outburst upset the players, for they knew well enough that Malcolm had not been given a new role in the side. He had not been told specifically to play deeper.

He went away to play in a testimonial game, and nothing was said when he returned on the Thursday, although we knew that one or two of his friends at the club had spoken to him. We didn't say anything that day, because we felt that the team meeting was the time to bring the matter up. When the issue was raised, Malcolm got his blow in first, as he told us that we were like sheep. He accused us of being afraid to stand up and speak our minds to his face, and said this was why he had gone into print.

There was a bit of an argument between Malcolm and

some of the players, while Gordon Lee stood back on the sidelines and said nothing. Possibly he felt that it was best for the players to thrash things out among themselves. Personally, at that stage, I still hoped that Malcolm would be the one who became converted, that he would contribute more and become part of a successful side.

In case anyone should get the impression that I was anti-Macdonald from the moment I arrived at Newcastle, let me say here and now that I never saw myself as a rival to 'Supermac', neither did I begrudge him the glory that his goals brought him. I would be less than honest, if I didn't say that even now, I still feel Malcolm is the best goal-scorer this country has seen since the days of Jimmy Greaves and Denis Law, and I'm certain that nothing upset Mal more than his omission from the England side. I would have thought that with almost 30 goals a season to his credit in domestic competition, he would have been an automatic choice for his country, and it amazes me that he isn't. At the same time, when I stop to think about it, maybe it boils down to a matter of teamwork and contribution to the team effort on the international scene, as well.

Shop talk during our break in Majorca didn't centre exclusively on 'Supermac'. The 1976 European Cup final in which Bayern Munich defeated St Etienne produced some real argument. Richard Dinnis had his supporters when he claimed Bayern hadn't deserved to win, because St Etienne were the better side, showing more genuine footballing flair and entertainment for the fans. Others of us argued that Bayern, by scoring one goal and not conceding any goals, had proved they were the better side. They had shown they could absorb punishment, then break away to score – and they had done the same thing against Leeds, the previous season.

Richard felt that this was a cynical way to view things, and in this respect, he was right. But, as professionals, we know we're under the constraints of the system which dictates the way we play and at the end of the day, success is the sole yardstick. Everyone wants to know the winners . . . no one wants to know the losers. The parallel at Newcastle was that, as one player said, 20 goals a season from a star striker wasn't sufficient to win the First Division championship . . . hence his assertion that Malcolm Macdonald really needed to double his scoring output to give Newcastle United the full value of his talent.

6 'Supermac'

Malcolm Macdonald has been meriting headline treatment for a few years now. Ever since the day he arrived at Newcastle in a limousine and, as a £180,000-valued striker, announced to the world that he was going to score goals galore. While he was at Newcastle, he was as good as his word, and he became the idol of thousands of supporters. He arrived in a blaze of publicity, and departed amid a furore of controversy. I was fortunate to be able to play alongside him as his striking partner, even if it was only for one full season, and it was an experience I wouldn't have missed for the world.

There is no getting away from it . . . 'Supermac' IS one of football's characters. When you have a striker who gets goals as regularly as Malcolm does, it's inevitable that he will attract attention and admiration, and command publicity, especially when he is not afraid to talk about his ability to tuck away the scoring chances. Labelled by many people as the most exciting striker in the country, Malcolm did his job. He said he had arrived to score goals, and he did – in season 1974–75, for instance, when he played in every one of United's League games, he found the net 21 times, and added another dozen goals in other competitive matches, while as an England striker, he scored five goals in one game at Wembley.

Malcolm was 'the man to whom defenders have to pay very special attention – but even then, they cannot stop him getting goals.' He was labelled on one occasion as 'priceless', although in the end, Arsenal, armed with a cheque for something like £330,000, proved otherwise.

Let's consider for a moment what makes the ideal centre-forward. He must have strength, aggression, speed, ball-control, and be prepared to run at defences. Which means he must also have courage, for once a striker gets into the 18-yard box, he will take the knocks. Above all, perhaps, a centre-forward must have a hunger for goals. As someone who knew what he was talking about summed up: 'When he looks up, the first thing he must be wanting to see is the goalposts of the opposing team – and then he must head for the target.'

The man who said that was Albert Stubbins, who totalled around 400 goals – an average of close on a goal a game – during his top-class career which took in spells with Liverpool and Newcastle United. With United, he scored no fewer than 265 goals in 199 matches, and his assessment of Malcolm Macdonald was this: 'I think he's just about the best in the country.' Albert also said: 'Malcolm loves to get goals . . . he's the old-fashioned centre-forward who goes straight for goal, and he packs a wallop – especially in that left foot.'

Kevin Keegan, who played alongside Malcolm for the first time in an international between England and West Germany, rated him as being 'different from anyone else I've ever played alongside . . . he's got a style of his own, and it's no use you trying to change that style. You've got to try to fit in. If he tried to change, he would lose his effectiveness. There's only one way he knows how to play, but he does it so well. To be a top striker, you have to be greedy, when it comes to shooting . . . and if he gets in four shots, the odds are that he'll score at least one goal.'

So 'Supermac' has talent. He also has bags of confidence in himself, and some people might argue that this confidence amounts to arrogance. On his transfer to Arsenal, Malcolm was saying – and I'm sure he believed it – that he would knock in 30 goals for his new club during the season. By the end of the season, he had justified his bold words, because he had finished as the First Division's joint top marksman, with 25 League goals, and 29 in all games.

Malcolm also had something to say about the difference between Arsenal and Newcastle, and he said it in his own, no-punches-pulled manner. 'In a word, it's respect.' In one way, he was right; in another, I would argue the point with him. Malcolm did have the respect of his Newcastle team-mates, because we all knew that he was good at his job. He was certainly right when he said: 'Eleven footballers don't have to like each other – merely have respect. There are players I don't necessarily like, but I know that if I'm in a sticky position on a Saturday, they'll be there alongside me, fighting it out. At Newcastle in my last season, they were only there if they liked you. If not – hard luck, mate. You were on your own.' And in another interview Malcolm made this complaint: 'The trouble is that for too long, Newcastle were hiding behind my goals.'

Malcolm Macdonald WAS a big name at Newcastle . . . but it takes more than one man to make a team. I found him extremely likeable as a person, though – he would sit and talk with you, like any other team-mate, and he was not short of words, when it came to expressing his views on football. Although he and I had to agree to differ, when it came to our respective outlooks on the game, I wouldn't find fault with him, for he is entitled to his opinions. I believe that, to a certain extent, he is in the game for personal glory, and there can be no doubting that he has made money from his various moves.

I think I'm more inclined towards the value of the team, as a team, than Malcolm is, but when we played together, we struck up a very good understanding, and the record book shows that our partnership worked. He got goals, and so did I – including hat-tricks against Wolves, Ipswich and Everton – and while some people claimed that Malcolm made my goals for me, this is a view which I cannot accept.

I firmly believe that in any partnership, one person complements the other, and that was how I saw my relationship with Malcolm. He might be the glamour boy, I might be the straight man – but together, we made holes in opposing defences. Frankly, in a way I think that it was a pity we had only one full season together, and far from Malcolm being the man who was the dominant factor, thereby having to play the leading role, let me say that if anyone was under pressure, it was myself – especially when, under questioning as to my ability, Gordon Lee went out on a limb and forecast that I would finish up with a higher tally of goals than Malcolm. Few managers would have ventured such a bold expression, and to this day I'm not quite sure if Gordon really believed it, or whether he was trying to gee the pair of us up But he turned out to be an accurate tipster, for while Mal scored 22 goals, I hit 31.

Off the field, I never had any quarrel with Mal, but if I'm honest I must say that when we were in the thick of the action, he didn't contribute as much in effort as other members of the side, including myself. Malcolm's answer to any and every criticism of his style was terse and to the point: 'Just put your goals on the table.' And his scoring record certainly stood scrutiny. But a Newcastle team-mate had a point, too, when he argued that if Malcolm were merely going to score goals, he would need to hit 40 a season to make up for lack of grafting and chasing.

There were many stories suggesting that Gordon Lee didn't take long to decide that Malcolm Macdonald was not one of the men who fitted in with his own ideas of teamwork, and this may have been so. My own impression is that Malcolm, in any event, had really had enough of Newcastle United, even before Gordon arrived. I think Malcolm felt that the time had come for him to move on to fresh pastures and, possibly, a new challenge. And if the pressure on Malcolm was greater, after Gordon Lee had taken charge of St James's Park, it was no easier for me when, after I had gone half a dozen matches without getting a goal, the manager said: 'Forget about Malcolm Macdonald . . . I'll bet Alan Gowling will score more goals.'

The sceptics reckoned the manager was daft, and I believe that when I topped the First Division scoring chart, it didn't go down too well with some of Malcolm's admirers in the crowd – after all, he was the idol of Tyneside, and the Geordie fans had become used to having their heroes. I suppose I was a bit of an upstart, hitting more goals than the local favourite.

Although rumour made it apparent that Malcolm and Gordon Lee were not seeing eye to eye, I never saw them get involved in any flare-up. Gordon, I'm certain, was very conscious that Malcolm was getting the major publicity (the manager wasn't overmuch concerned with his own image), and Gordon wanted to be able to talk about everyone in his side, and not just about one star player. That, perhaps, was why, when he was being questioned about 'Supermac' and my failure to get goals, he answered: 'Forget Malcolm Macdonald . . . what about Alan Gowling?'

There were no dressing-room arguments between manager and star; there was no open hostility. It didn't appear to be an abrasive relationship, and so far as I could judge, the pair of them developed a working basis, tolerating each other because each had a job to do. I wouldn't know if Malcolm respected Gordon as a manager, although I'm pretty certain he respected him for his intense enthusiasm and interest in everything. Certainly Gordon respected Malcolm's ability to get goals – but I think he felt this alone didn't make for a consistently winning team.

Despite the fact that Gordon Lee took Newcastle and Everton to League Cup finals in successive seasons, he wasn't and isn't what you could call a 'Cup' manager. He used to say that Cups were tin-pot trophies; for him, the League title was the supreme prize. And to win that, you needed a team of 11 men, all of them 90-minute triers, as well as having the accomplishments which must go with the all-round effort.

It's difficult to know how much opposition, if any, there was from the boardroom when it came to selling Malcolm. I suspect that in a way, there was relief that the burden could fall squarely on Gordon's slim shoulders. If a player and his manager don't see eye to eye, if the player is already in the mood to pick up his boots and travel on, and if the manager believes that this would be best for the club and the team, then you have only one problem: what about the paying customers, the fans who idolise the player? – This is a sticky one for the directors who realise that by letting the player go, they are inviting the wrath of thousands of people. But if it becomes plain that there is no acceptable alternative, then you are helped in your dilemma by being able to say there was no other solution to the problem, and hope that people will soon get over the shock.

Malcolm made it crystal-clear how he was feeling when, at the Press day for photographs, he refused to appear – he didn't want to be on the team picture, because he couldn't raise a smile. It was clear, then, that it was only a matter of time before he shook the dust of Newcastle from his boots. That incident, just as surely, was another nail in the coffin, so far as the relationship between player and manager was concerned. Not long afterwards, Malcolm joined Arsenal. When I learned about the move, he had already gone with Arsenal manager Terry Neill to London – I found out about the deal having been finalised when I read the sports pages. Newcastle had collected more than £300,000, and the Geordie fans had lost their superstar.

The players who remained were only too well aware of what the supporters were saying . . . that United had transfered their greatest asset. The fans threatened to boycott the matches, and for a time the attendance figures dipped. But the players' attitude was determined: 'Now we can set about showing that we're NOT a one-man team.' Our own pride was at stake, apart from the fact that we wanted to do well for Gordon Lee, whose head had to be on the block. There were no dramatic statements or proclamations of faith, just a desire to get on with the job. People outside the club might be talking of Newcastle being relegated, now that United had sold their goal-scoring machine. But among the players, not one voice was raised in protest.

I must admit that before our first match, after Malcolm's departure, the players were a little apprehensive as to the sort of reception we would get from the fans. I sensed that the supporters were a bit apprehensive, as well, as to how we would fare. But we won our first match, against Sheffield United in the Anglo-Scottish tournament, and I scored twice when we followed up by beating Middlesbrough. By the Christmas, we felt we were winning over the fans, and we were looking not over our shoulders, but forward to the exciting challenge of what was to come. We had grown in confidence and composure, be-lieving that we were well on the way to becoming a team which could acquit itself well in every game, and not just on isolated occasions.

Then came the freeze-up, and we were able to play only one match in the space of about a month. And there arose another problem, this time concerning the future of Gordon Lee, who was being tipped as a likely successor to Billy Bingham at Everton. We could read the signs, for apart from paper talk, there were indications that Gordon wasn't his old self. He was becoming short-tempered and edgy, and it showed after we had lost a game at Derby, for there was one hell of a bust-up in the dressing-room, and I was the central character.

The flare-up was sparked off about my having been de-tailed to keep watch on Derby centre-half Roy McFarland, when we were defending at corner kicks. As had hap-pened when Malcolm Macdonald was detailed to watch Duncan McKenzie against Leeds, MacFarland had 'lost' me and scored for Derby. After the game, I accepted im-mediately that the mistake was mine, and having acknow-ledged as much, I couldn't see what else there was to add. The damage had been done.

Completely out of character for him, Gordon Lee kept harping on about my mistake, and he also kept on talking about mistakes other players had made. Apart from my own error, I was feeling upset about the way we had played – or failed to play – as a team on that occasion, and one thing led to another until there was a real verbal battle in progress, with Gordon and myself in the thick of the argument. At the back of my mind, I thought that perhaps he was suffering from the pressure at boardroom level, but later I realised that it was obviously because the Everton job had become available, and he knew that he was in line for it. So he was probably concerned, more than anything, with the problems of trying to decide which way to move, and this strain showed in the way he reacted after the defeat at Derby.

By the time we got back to Newcastle the incident was virtually over and done with, but as we got down to training one day shortly afterwards, we were surprised to see one of the Newcastle United directors running – yes, I said running – across and calling to Gordon. He told our manager that the chairman, Lord Westwood, would like to see him. And that, to us, was the clearest sign of all that events were about to happen.

Gordon left the training session, saw the chairman, and when he returned, he pulled three of the players – skipper Geoff Nulty, Mickey Burns and myself – on one side. He told us what we had already guessed: that Everton had made an approach, though he didn't yet know if he were going to take the job. He asked if we thought he should tell the rest of the players, and we said that as they had already guessed what was going on, there seemed no point in secrecy. So the playing staff heard the news officially.

The following Saturday, Newcastle United were playing Manchester City in the fifth round of the FA Cup at St James's Park, and by then the betting was that over the week-end, Gordon Lee would be named as the new manager of Everton. The surprising thing about it all, to me, was that the Newcastle players didn't regard it as any sort of betrayal on Gordon's part; they all understood the pres-

sures under which he had been working, and they felt that
for his own peace of mind, he would find greater reward –
and not just financially – in making the move to Everton.
His family were still living in Lancashire, and that fact
alone must have been a great pull for him.

On the Saturday, there was an air of expectancy and
tension, as we went out to do battle with Manchester City.
Naturally, the United players wanted to round off Gordon's
managerial career at St. James's Park with a victory
flourish; but we couldn't produce the form of which we
were capable, and we went out of the Cup. Over the
week-end, Gordon met the Everton officials, and within
48 hours he was installed as the new manager at Goodison
Park. Despite our genuine sadness at his going, we didn't
press for him to stay. We felt that he had been knocking his head against a brick wall for 18 months, although
this was denied in discussions we had later with the
directors.

There was an ironic ending to the Gordon Lee era
at Newcastle, for – as had happened when he left Blackburn – there were some bitter exchanges after he had
moved on again. As Everton were preparing to appoint
him, the Newcastle chairman was talking of United seeking compensation for the loss of 'the best manager in
England'. Lord Westwood said Newcastle would expect to
receive compensation 'over and above what Gordon's contract is worth. We had to do this with Blackburn, when
he came here.'

Gordon, it was said, still had 18 months of his contract
to run at Newcastle, and it was suggested that his salary
would leap from £12,000 to £20,000 a year, once he had
moved in at Everton. It was further suggested in the newspapers that Newcastle would be looking for £12,000 on
top of the money required to 'buy up' Gordon's contract,

which meant that there would be a £30,000 'fee' on his head. Gordon made it clear at the time of his leaving how he felt. 'Everton are a very ambitious club, and I'm an ambitious man. The trump card is that my family are in Lancashire, so I will be going home.'

One of the interesting things which emerged from all the controversy surrounding Gordon's move to Everton was a suggestion that there should be a transfer fee put on the heads of managers under contract. Former Manchester United manager Tommy Docherty made the point in an interview at the time with the *Manchester Evening News*. He reckoned that there should be 'a real, hefty payment on the lines of the kind of six-figure transfer fee that would be paid for a star player.' His argument was that 'there are too many clubs . . . who are getting into trouble and then seeking their salvation by pinching some more successful club's boss.'

He made a telling point when he emphasised that it would be 'a restraint of trade, and unfair to individual managers, if you tried to make it impossible for managers to switch clubs', but said it would be logical if a club seeking a manager had to pay for the privilege of getting a team boss who was under contract elsewhere. Instancing the case of Gordon Lee, he said: 'Everton worried a few clubs, before they decided Gordon was their man. You couldn't blame him for wanting to take up the offer, be it to better himself or return to Lancashire to link up with his family again. For all I know, Everton might have paid Newcastle some compensation, but I bet it wasn't the kind of £100,000 cash I am thinking about.' And then: 'Perhaps Newcastle couldn't expect too much, because Blackburn Rovers claim they had to go to law to get compensation when they lost Lee to Newcastle.'

Irrespective of how Newcastle United might have felt

about losing Gordon, the Newcastle players didn't want to lose him, even if they didn't present a petition for him to stay. They believed he must do what he felt to be best in his own interests. I do agree with Newcastle and with Tommy Docherty that when a club finds it is about to lose a manager who is under contract, it is entitled to receive compensation. But I think that if the club receives full payment for the remainder of his contract, then that should be considered a satisfactory solution.

7 Tempers Rise Again

Footballers can be, and are, serious. They can be serious about football and politics, and other topics that are of concern to other groups of people, but they do find it difficult to maintain their serious conversation for long. There is always someone to turn the situation back to a more mundane level, with a funny interjection. Footballers like to talk, but they prefer to keep it simple, rather than philosophical. Like other work groups, they prefer to discuss the virtues of the 'bird' in the office or who appears in the daily paper. They catch up on each other's activities of the previous night, who went where and with whom and for what! They will discuss TV programmes, especially those of a more escapist or comical nature, or a sexy play. Similarly, with films their preference is more escapism.

However, footballers like to talk about football most. In this respect, their interest is total. They will cover every aspect of football in the season of conversation. They will discuss topics in the news regarding football.

They will discuss any matches that they may have seen on TV or live, covering details of their thoughts on the game, who played well, what they thought of the ref, or what they thought of the match commentator, if the game was on TV. They will talk about players at other clubs, discussing their virtues or some incident involving them in the past. They will talk about managers and trainers, including their own. They will criticise or praise them, in turn.

Footballers rarely form a social group as a whole, and rarely do they all go out together. There are occasions when a large number of players can be seen out together, but even these are few and far between. It may be a Christmas drink or a bachelor night. The usual case is for players to pursue their activities in small groups of three or four, or occasionally two of these groups might join for a night out in a disco or a drink after a game. On the whole, though, the numbers are small. Possibly once in a lifetime do they band together to make a stand because they all feel the same way about something which affects their lives and their careers. This happened at Newcastle United, after Gordon Lee had made his exit from St James's Park.

Under him, there had developed a tremendous team spirit. His departure left the players in limbo, for a little while. But we were all anxious about one thing – that the team spirit which had been fostered should not be allowed to crumble and fade away. Everyone was convinced that we were moving along the right lines, that we were capable of making futher progress and becoming a really successful side. So it came as something of a relief when three of us – captain Geoff Nulty, Mickey Burns and myself – were invited to go and see the chairman, Lord Westwood, at his home. It meant that we could at least put our views forward to the people at the top.

With the chairman, when we arrived, was another director, Stan Seymour, junior. We were asked for our opinions, as we had hoped would be the case, and we told the two officials that we felt Richard Dinnis should be given the chance to continue along the lines laid down by Gordon Lee, and along which he had worked in conjunction with

Gordon. To us, that seemed a logical thing. The chairman took note of our request, and intimated that Richard would be given the job of handling team affiairs. There were three of us at the meeting with the two directors, and when we came out, each one of us was under no mis-apprehension as to what we had heard . . . we all agreed that we felt Richard Dinnis was going to get the job.

We reported the result of our interview to the rest of the players, who were in agreement with our viewpoint, and said that it looked as if Dick would be named man-ager. But that didn't turn out to be the case, for when an announcement was made, Dick was put in charge of team affairs and team selection. But he was not confirmed as the manager.

Possibly to people outside the game, the name of Richard Dennis meant nothing, for he was a comparative new-comer to the professional football scene. He is in his middle 30's, has spent more years in teaching than in professional football, and never played Soccer as a professional. But he has a diploma in physical education, has been a fully-qualified FA coach for more than a dozen years, and started his career when Jimmy Adamson, then the manager at Burnley, gave him a job on a part-time basis look-ing after the youngsters at Turf Moor. Next, he gave up his teaching job to go coaching at Blackburn Rovers, and when Gordon Lee left for Newcastle, he was one of the candidates to succeed him at Ewood Park. But after act-ing as caretaker manager, he moved again, and followed Gordon to St James's Park.

It was a gamble, when Dick Dinnis joined the backroom staff at Newcastle United, because for a start, he wasn't on contract and, therefore, he steadfastly refused to up-root his family from their home in Lancashire. Like Gordon Lee, he spent a considerable time living out of a suitcase, staying in an hotel during the week and visiting his family at the week-end. No contract meant that there was no real security, yet it says much for Richard Dinnis that he wanted to prove he could go into the world of the professionals and make the grade with them.

He wasn't exactly one of the highest-paid men on the backroom side of the game, and there were times when he seriously considered if he should forget about a career in professional football, and return to the security of teaching. I have told how, during the first season or so, he was very much on the sidelines. He explained it another way: 'I was no more than a lackey, collecting loose balls at training sessions. That got me down. I desperately wanted to become involved at first-team level.'

Gordon Lee finally brought him into the scheme of things, at first-team level, and he showed he could cope with the demands. He did admit that he had had 'something of a hang-up about how First Division players would look upon a coach who had never played the game above the level of Blackburn Rovers reserves – and never as a professional.' But he found what I found: that players will accept you, in the end, if you are strong and decisive, and if they realise that you have something to contribute to the cause of the team.

Richard admitted, also: 'I have accepted that there were things they could teach me. A good coach listens and observes as he talks.' He listened, observed, learned – and gained the respect of the players.

When we realised that he was not being confirmed as the manager, we held a players' meeting, and it would be foolish of me to deny it – some heated words were spoken. But Richard, who attended the meeting, played his part in cooling the atmosphere, and initial talk of strike action was forgotten. We did decide to issue a statement, and this took some time to prepare, because at first some of the players wanted to word the statement extremely strongly, and it required some persuasion before we set the right tone, in terms which were acceptable to everyone.

The statement recognised the right of the directors to select whoever they wished as manager. We were very conscious of the words 'player power', and the misuse of position. We didn't want to lay ourselves open to accusations of 'player power', but we were unanimous in our desire to show the directors what we truly felt. It was obvious to us that Richard's position was going to be reviewed, and the pressure was on us. We went to play at Bristol City, and we came away with a 1–1 draw . . . a satisfactory performance, considering that our away record had not been one of the best.

We were given the following Monday off, and when we reported on the Tuesday morning for training, the first thing we heard was that Newcastle United had signed a player named Ralph Callachan from Hearts. I got the news in a phone call from a Pressman, who asked me if I would comment on the fact that the club had signed the player without Richard Dinnis knowing anything about the deal going through. I'm not daft enough to comment on something I know nothing about, so I politely, but firmly, declined to say anything.

However, when the rest of the players learned what had happened, there were some more heated words said, as tempers rose even higher than at the first meeting.

It became plain that the patience of the players generally was being taxed to the utmost, and the overall feeling was that the directors had interfered in an area which should be the manager's prerogative. It could have been argued, possibly, that Richard Dinnis was not, in fact, the manager, but he was certainly in charge of team affairs, so any distinction must of necessity be a very fine one, indeed. And not only that, but at the least it was discourteous not to have informed the man in charge of the players what was happening.

The players felt, also, that they had done a considerable amount of work off the field to improve the image of the club. They had attended functions, visited hospitals, and generally done their best to give the people who supported Newcastle United the feeling that this really was their team, one which they could support with confidence.

There can be no doubt about it, to my way of thinking: Richard Dinnis should have been consulted about the signing of a new player – any new player. It was unfortunate for Ralph Callachan that he was the man involved, and no one blamed him for what had happened, but Richard had been made to look a nonentity, and to say that he was hopping mad about the position in which he had found himself is to state nothing less than the truth.

He went to see the chairman, to establish his position at the club . . . and, at the same time, the players got together again and issued another statement. All the players in the first-team pool, bar David Craig (who was injured and could not be contacted) were present, and once again, there was some strong talk about strike action. But again, saner counsels prevailed, and it was made clear that such a drastic step was out of the question.

So it was decided to issue another statement to show all the people of Newcastle that the players were not in agreement with the action which had been taken, and we made the thing quite simple and crystal-clear . . . the players had no confidence in the board of directors, and they were saying this publicly.

Richard Dinnis was at home in bed that night when,

close to midnight, he received a call to go and see the chairman. When he had dressed and gone to the chairman's house, he discovered that he was being offered a contract which named him as acting manager, and that this contract would run until June 30, 1977. It thus became clear that the influence which the players had wielded had, in fact, defused a potentially explosive situation, because the urgency of the midnight meeting with the chairman had brought about a positive confirmation of where Richard Dinnis stood.

Richard himself appreciated that he had the backing of the players. 'They have paid me the best compliment possible by wanting me as Gordon Lee's successor. To have that kind of support is very heart-warming,' he said afterwards. 'I don't like the phrase "player-power" – I prefer "player influence." The only people with real power in football are directors, the men with the power to hire and fire. But players do have influence, and that's how it should be.

'Newcastle's have been genuinely concerned about the choice of a man to follow Gordon Lee. Their motives have been of the best. They have said and done everything with the best interests of the club at heart. This is an intelligent dressing-room, containing some of the brightest thinkers in the game. I have to be flattered – and grateful – that they rate me highly enough to want me as the boss.'

Dick confessed that, after his difficult start on the backroom side at Newcastle, 'one of the most rewarding things of my life has been my rapport with the Newcastle squad.' He was realistic enough to add that 'This will not necessarily make me a successful acting manager in terms of points, but it's comforting to know that players have as much respect for you as you have for them.

'I would be a fool to imagine our problems are over,

just because I have been placed in charge for the moment. Harsh words have been spoken on both sides, and I'm not naive enough to believe that all will be forgiven and forgotten overnight. But footballers are basically interested in getting on with training and playing. In general terms, they have no wish to involve themselves with anything else. The Newcastle players have become involved because they care genuinely. They feel a lot of progress has been made in the last season and a half. They want it to be maintained.'

Once the club had given him the job of acting manager to the end of the season, with the possibility of keeping the job if the team did well, we all got down to showing that we could pull together. Richard summed it up when he said: 'We proved up to Christmas that we were one of the most formidable teams in the country. Togetherness and teamwork were our strengths. We have to settle back to that pattern quickly. It won't be easy, but nothing could be more distracting than the events of the past fortnight or so. Now I'm sitting in what I've been told is the least-wanted managerial seat in the game. But it's mine for the present, and I shall do my best to occupy it with some dignity and, hopefully, some success.'

It is interesting to see how Newcastle's results went, during the time that Richard Dinnis was in charge, towards the end of season 1976–77. We lost, 3–1, against Manchester United at Old Trafford, scored a 2–0 victory over Tottenham at St James's Park, and by doing so, moved up from 10th place in the table to eighth. We had also played four matches fewer than several of the teams in the First Division, because of the winter freeze-up, so this meant that we were in a position where, if we got the right results, we could finish in a position high enough to enable Newcastle United to qualify for a place in Europe the following season.

Liverpool beat us by the only goal of the game at Anfield (and by the end of the season, they had remained undefeated, winning 18 games and dropping only three points on their own ground); we stuck five goals past Norwich City at St James's Park and got a 1–1 draw at West Brom, then won 2–1 at Birmingham; we failed to score in a home draw against Leicester City, but gave West Ham a 3–0 hiding; then we went to Loftus-road and beat Queen's Park Rangers by the odd goal in three. Unhappily for us, we came unstuck when the next visitors arrived at St James's Park . . . Arsenal, who scored two goals without reply. And Malcolm Macdonald got their first goal!

We also lost 2–0 against champion-challenging Ipswich Town at Portman-road, but wound up with a 3–2 victory over League Cup winners Aston Villa at St James's Park, to leave ourselves with one game to go, and 49 points in the bag. Above us were League-champions Liverpool, runners-up Manchester City, and third-placed Ipswich. Below us, Manchester United and Aston Villa were still in a position to overtake us, and rob us of fourth place in the final table. But to do that, United would have had to make it a cricket score in their final match at West Ham (which they lost), so really, it was between us and Villa. They won their last game, we lost at Everton. But we had finished fifth and were in Europe.

Judged by any standard, this was a pretty impressive performance for a team which had suffered more than one traumatic experience during the season, losing one manager the players respected, having to fight for another they also respected and, thereby, putting pressure on themselves, with the knowledge that they were going into each game looking for points which would enable Richard Dinnis to keep his job on a much more stable basis.

We had taken some drastic measures, to make our feelings known to the directors and to the public of Newcastle. Equally, it had been a drastic move to call Richard Dinnis from his bed.

Throughout the season, supporters had had several meetings with one or two directors, and there was the culminating extraordinary general meeting, which was closed to the Press. But the news leaked out that the directors had not given an unqualified 'Yes' to the appointment of Dick Dinnis as manager, when his contract expired on June 30. So at that stage, it remained a case of wait and see.

Facts cannot be blinked, and to the players it seemed, at various stages of the season, that there were some directors who, to put it mildly, were not pulling the same way as ourselves. Their aims and ours, it appeared, were not necessarily the same. They were non-committal about giving Richard the contract we felt he had earned, and they didn't think they were doing anything wrong by prevaricating.

In fairness, they probably felt just as strongly that we should not get involved in matters which, from their standpoint, were not really our concern. The chairman had some time earlier set up a committee so that views could be aired – let me point out that the Commission on Industrial Relations advised such a committee at every club – and the members were the chairman, Stan Seymour, junior, Geoff Nulty, myself and (at that time) Gordon Lee. But events had moved on apace.

I will say that once Richard was named as the man in charge for the rest of the season, we set out our stall accordingly, for we knew that we had to improve upon an abysmal away record – and we did just that. We discussed the matter fully, and made what might be called a policy decision. We determined to concentrate during away matches on getting more men behind the ball; it might not look pretty, at times, but we judged it was necessary and hoped it would prove effective. It worked well, for we scored a few victories, as well as putting a clamp on games. You have to start somewhere, and it was important not to lose, until we could acquire the confidence which would enable us to go out looking for victory in every game we played.

And so far as our actions off the field were concerned, all the way along the line we had to be sure that we were being seen to be doing the right thing. We were conscious of the fact that our contracts tied us to the club, conscious of the legal aspects of the situation, conscious that we should not lay ourselves open to charges of 'player-power' and attempted dictatorship. I think that we succeeded.

We wanted the good work Gordon Lee and Richard Dinnis had done to continue, because we felt it had begun to show some sort of success, in terms of constistency – which is the overall target for any team aspiring to honours. Bear in mind, also, that security is one of the greatest factors in a player's career . . . and no one wanted to see the fruits of 18 months' work going down the drain, and to feel that we had lost all sense of direction. By the end of the season, when Newcastle United's players, under Richard Dinnis, had done well enough to qualify for Europe, the club recognised what we had achieved by offering Richard a two-year contract. That, I believe, spoke for itself.

8 No Way Could I Shed Tears

My old Manchester United team-mate, goalkeeper Alex Stepney, revealed to the world how footballers can be affected by incidents which mark the high spots or the low points of their careers. Just before he went to Wembley with Manchester United for the second successive season, in the spring of 1977, he told millions of television viewers how he broke down emotionally, after United had won the European Cup in 1968, and how he had managed to bottle up his feelings after United had lost the 1976 FA Cup final against Southampton.

On that occasion, the TV cameras swooped in for a close-up of United centre-half Brian Greenoff, stunned and in tears after their defeat; they also captured for all time that engaging wink which the Saint's manager, Lawrie McMenemy, gave on Cup-final day, just as they caught the grimly grey expression on the face of Bolton manager Ian Greaves, as he suffered the tensions of watching his team play in a vital match. The cameras were not there, as Manchester United made their way home sadly from the 1976 FA Cup final, but Alex Stempney candidly admitted how he felt, and what happened.

In the dressing-room after the game, he managed to remain stoical, despite his deep, hurting feeling of disappointment. He was United's senior player, and he was trying to help the younger players by showing that he could mask his feelings.

Ray Clemence, the Liverpool goalkeeper who has yet to concede a goal against me, traced his Wembley experiences – and he has been there a few times now – back to the FA Cup final of 1971. He revealed that as he came out of the tunnel, and emerged into the daylight to hear the roar of 100,000 people, he felt for a moment like turning back and fleeing into the obscurity he had just left.

Manchester City skipper Mike Doyle, who is one of the few players I have known who seem to possess no nerves, even on the biggest of occasions, has spoken about the 1976 League Cup final as a game where his team had the feeling of mastery over Newcastle, just as Liverpool always seemed to have the edge in the FA Cup final of 1974, when Newcastle United didn't really do themselves justice.

You can believe me when I say that players, individually, feel deeply about things in the game, even though they may try to hide those feelings from the outside world. There is nothing better for a player than to go out on the pitch full of confidence and feeling the adrenalin flowing. Each individual prepares himself in his own way. Some players like to think about the game for some time beforehand, building themselves, up; others prefer not to think about the game at all, until the final moments, wishing to go out on the field in a relaxed state of mind. Some players like to be in the dressing-room early, others prefer to play cards in the team coach until the last possible moment.

In the same way, different players can take the blows of football in different ways. When you've just won a trophy, especially for the first time, there is not the slightest doubt about your emotions – you are delighted, and you don't care how much you let your feelings show. But sometimes, your joy can be tempered with restraint – as for, instance, the Liverpool players' joy of winning the League championship in season 1976–77 was tempered by the knowledge that they were still striving to win the FA Cup and the European Cup, as well. As Steve Highway put it: 'You had the feeling that you hadn't really achieved anything, unless you got at least one of the other two trophies, as well.'

Liverpool's defeat by Manchester United in the FA Cup final was mirrored in their faces as they walked off the pitch, and in what they said afterwards. They needed to be picked up, mentally and physically, for the European final. To quote Steve Highway again, this time on the match in Rome, and the effect the Liverpool fans had on their team: 'They gave us an electric charge when we came out on the pitch that left us tingling from head to toe right through to the finish.' Liverpool conquered Burussia Moenchengladbach decisively, and the contrast in their emotions was plain, when you reflected how they had felt the previous Saturday at Wembley.

I have known the ups and downs, too. It was a terrible feeling at Huddersfield to realise that despite all your efforts, you had just slipped out of the Second Division and into the Third – and even worse, two years later, to lose Third Division status and drop into the very bottom league of all. You feel sorry for the manager, you feel sorry for your team-mates . . . most of all, you feel bitterly sorry for yourself.

It's a grim feeling, as you get back into the dressing-room. No one wants to talk, no one wants to look at anyone else – least of all look at the picture of misery the manager's face presents, for you know it probably mirrors your own. You just sit down wearily on the bench, staring into space. You don't even think about the disillusioned supporters, drifting away silently, as if from a funeral.

You sit there, thinking: 'It's happened to us – to ME. Bloody hell . . .'

Ian Greaves knew the joy of taking Huddersfield Town into the First Division, the grim despair of going down with them to the Second and the Third. When he moved to Bolton, he had the horrible experience – and I use the word 'horrible' advisedly – of seeing his side just miss promotion in successive seasons. It is at such times that a manager perhaps begins to wonder about his own part in the scheme of things, to ask himself if he's a 'jonah'. As Ian said, you start to try to find reasons for the failure, and you could put it down to many things – you could even blame it on the players' strip not being washed the right way. But you know it boils down simply to the fact that the promoted teams finished up with more points than yours.

Wembley was a completely new experience for me, and when Newcastle United won their League Cup semi-final against Spurs, the Magpies' dressing-room was a scene of sheer delight. It seemed too good to believe, and the feeling of euphoria was almost unreal. You were somewhere on a cloud. Newcastle lost the League Cup final against Manchester City, but I was fortunate, because I just couldn't bring myself to feel too disappointed. Why not? – At the back of my mind there was the knowledge that only 12 months earlier I had been about to turn my back on the game, rather than sink to oblivion in the Fourth Division. When you've suffered an experience like that, the chance of going to Wembley is reward in itself, and although I wished we could have won, there was no way I could shed tears. What's more, on my first visit, I had scored a goal.

Newcastle, like the rest of the big clubs, by-passed the first round, and were paired with Southport in the second.

They said they would rather play at St James's Park, and have the money, than try conclusions with us on their own, Haig-avenue ground. Naturally, we didn't object too strenuously, because we felt that in front of our own supporters, we should get through easily enough.

Southport got what they deserved, in one respect, for there was a gate of more than 23,500 at St James's Park, which far eclipsed the crowd they could have expected at Haig-avenue. In another way, they also got what they might have expected, for we ran riot, scoring six goals without reply. Young striker Paul Cannell, playing in place of the injured Malcolm Macdonald, scored two of the goals, and I got the other four.

The third round, and we were drawn away again. This time our opponents, Bristol Rovers, had no qualms about the game going on at their ground, so we had to travel to Eastville. More than 17,000 people turned up, and when Bristol Rovers were leading at half-time, it looked as if there might be a turn-up for the book. But I managed to score an equaliser in the second half, and so we went home happy to have got a replay.

Tommy Craig scored from the penalty spot, and Irving Nattrass got another goal, so the 25,000 fans who had come to watch the replay at St James's Park went home happy. And in the fourth round, we came up against First Division opposition for the first time – Queen's Park Rangers – and once again we were drawn away. So if we did finally make it to Wembley, no one could say we had had it easy.

We went to Loftus-road, and scored one of the best victories of the round, sticking three goals past Rangers, in reply to the one they got. Our marksmen were Malcolm Macdonald, Mickey Burns and Geoff Nulty. And with the fifth round looming, we began to have visions of a date

D

at Wembley . . . especially when we were paired against
Notts County, and had the advantage of being at home for
a change. But it took a strange goal, indeed, for Newcastle
to emerge the winners, and we breathed a sigh of real
relief, when it was all over. So did the 31,000 Geordie
fans who had spent 90 minutes sweating it out with us.

The goal came when Malcolm Macdonald took one
of his famous long throws, and the ball sailed right into
the Notts County goalmouth. Their 'keeper looked as if
he were all set to collect it cleanly, then he fumbled – and
the ball fell from his grasp and dropped down to my
knees. As it fell, it bounced against my chest . . . and
bobbled over the County goal line. One of the County
defenders was on the spot to whip the ball away, but
there was no doubt about it – his rescue act came too late.
The ball had gone over the line, and it was a goal to
Gowling.

The stories were circulating before the game that if we
didn't win this one, manager Gordon Lee was in line for
trouble, with his job at stake; so we had every reason
to be grateful for that in-off goal of mine. Maybe the
rumours were true, maybe not . . . but we had won, and
no one could do anything dramatic after that. We were in
the semi-finals, and just 180 minutes away from Wembley,
for the next stage of the League Cup competition was a
two-legged affair.

By then, we had started out on the trail of the FA Cup,
as well, and there was to be plenty of incident in that
competition before we had finished. For a time, indeed,
we thought that we might be going to Wembley in both
competitions, but it wasn't to be. Still, we did make it
in the League Cup, and I'm sure that Spurs, our semi-
final opponents, felt their defeat even more keenly than
when we went out of the FA Cup against Derby County.

More than 40,000 people flocked to White Hart-lane for this League Cup clash of First Division giants, both of whom had earned reputations through the years as Cup fighters. Spurs seemed to win every time they reached Wembley – and they had been there a few times; Newcastle were reviving memories of those three visits to the stadium by the FA Cup-fighting teams of the 1950's.

The first leg finished with Tottenham having gained the upper hand – but only just. They knew after 90 minutes that they had to travel to St James's Park and protect a one goal lead, or try to add to it and risk being caught stretched. In the first game, which was very even, their 'keeper, Pat Jennings, had saved their bacon when he made a tremendous stop from Tommy Craig. In the return match, Newcastle were on level terms only two minutes after we had kicked off, for I stuck the ball in the net. I took a flick on from Malcolm Macdonald, and although Spurs defenders thought I was offside, I played to the whistle – which never came.

On I went, until only Pat Jennings stood between myself and the target, and as he advanced from his goal, I took the ball round him and stabbed it into the empty net. Geoff Nulty made it 2–1 on aggregate for us, in the second half, and Glen Keeley headed a third goal for Newcastle, so although Spurs defender Don McAllister pulled one back, it was not enough to prevent us going through to the final.

I was thrilled to bits. The previous year, I had been to Wembley as a spectator, to watch Norwich City and Aston Villa in the final of the League Cup, but I had never dreamed then that 12 months later, I would be looking forward to playing there in the final. Especially with the fortunes of Huddersfield Town, my club at that time, at such a low ebb. Now, it was all coming up roses . . .

although the FA Cup was proving to be a marathon affair. For we had been paired with Bolton Wanderers, managed by my old boss, Ian Greaves.

His team were also going for promotion to the First Division, so they were chasing a double target. Newcastle were going to Wembley in the League Cup, and hoping to make it there in the FA Cup, as well. The ingredients were there for a thriller – and a thriller it turned out to be.

Six goals were shared in the meeting between the teams at Burnden Park, and that meant a replay at St James's Park. This time, neither side could manage even one goal, so the caravan got under way again, with Elland-road the venue for the decider. The traffic was nose to tail along the motorway as vehicles from Newcastle and Bolton converged and headed slowly for the exit to the ground. Our coach got jammed in the thick of this stream, and finally the driver managed to pull over on to the hard shoulder and somehow get through, so that we got to the ground on time.

The second replay was being staged on the Monday of League Cup-final week, and it was a tough thing for both teams, since we had a final coming up, while Bolton were coming to the run-in of their promotion campaign. Yet once again, every player gave it all he'd got; there was total commitment in the decider at Elland-road. And at the end, we had just sneaked through, by the odd goal in three. Oddly enough, never once during those three matches against Bolton did Ian Greaves or I exchange a word – I think we were both too wrapped up in our respective ambitions of finding a way out of the Cup-tie impasse. And when it was all over, both sides, to put it bluntly, were buggered. Bolton, indeed, missed promotion, and Newcastle went out against Derby County in the next round of the FA Cup.

We had some scares, too, just before the final of the League Cup, for we knew, for one thing, that our skipper, Geoff Nulty would be an absentee from the side at Wembley, since he had fractured his jaw. Then, in League Cup-final week, one player after another at Newcastle went down with flu, and for a couple of days or so it became doubtful if we would be able to field a team. On the day, several of our players turned out still feeling under 100 per cent fit, and I still remain convinced that the flu bug, and the injury to Geoff, contributed as much as anything Manchester City did towards our 2–1 defeat.

There was no doubt that apart from some players not being able to stay the pace, we missed the inspiring influence of Geoff as captain, as well as his ability as a player. And as if to emphasise that misfortunes never come singly, almost immediately the final was over, I became a victim of the flu bug, and I felt extremely ill for several days.

It's amazing how people can have varying fortunes. Ron Saunders, for instance, never seems to be away from Wembley as the manager of a League Cup-final team . . . he has made four trips to the final in five years. Steve Heighway has been to Wembley three times in seven years with Liverpool, and has collected three League-championship and three European medals, as well. Ian Greaves has twice seen his Bolton side pipped at the post for promotion, and Gordon Lee has twice steered a team to Wembley in the League Cup and seen his men lose the final each time.

Maybe Gordon will make it third-time lucky, and maybe Alan Gowling will return to the ground where he once played in a five-a-side game, behind closed doors, nine years before making his one and only appearance there in front of 100,000 people. For in 1968, on the eve of the

European Cup final between Manchester United and Benfica, the players of both sides were allowed a sneak preview of the famous turf, and each club was allowed to do 30 minutes' training on the Wembley pitch. That's how I came to be playing in that five-a-side. But when the European Cup final began for real, I was on the sidelines.

But though I was disappointed in 1976, I don't regret having gone to Wembley with Newcastle and finishing on the losing side . . . playing there is one of the summits of a footballer's ambitions, and when I think that I appeared at Wembley in a Cup final, it gives me a glow. You don't easily forget things like that, when you've been so close to going out of football.

9 Getting a Laugh Out of Life

Players' humour is earthy, sometimes sarcastic. In a career where the tensions often show, it's good to take every opportunity of getting a laugh out of life. So players are always looking for a laugh, telling jokes, looking for slips by other people in speech or names. They'll tell stories about anyone and everyone – but they don't particularly like telling a joke that rebounded on themselves. Players are human, too.

One player at a club had a reputation for getting his words mixed up, and it raised a laugh one day when he answered the phone at the training ground and said to someone on the other end of the line who, obviously, was feeling worked up about something: 'Hey, calm down . . . I don't know what you're getting so historical about!" Then there was the story going the rounds which had nothing to do with football, but it was good for a laugh. 'Did you hear the one about the Irishman who fell through the window ironing his curtains?'

One aspect of conversation between players repeats itself time and time again. That's the anecdote. There's always someone who is ready to tell a story, usually regarded as funny, about what happened to someone else or what it was like at such-and-such a club, where the chairman was a twit or the manager a right bastard. 'I remember in the old days,' one senior professional will say. 'We never used to see a ball after Tuesday. The manager believed that come Saturday, everyone would be wanting the ball. But by the time Saturday came round, we'd forgotten what the bloody ball looked like."

Another will chip in: 'Hey, what about the time So-and-so was here! Remember when we were doing shooting practice one day, and he was told to take the ball up to Jim, play a one-two, and he did this then he got to the box and turned to ask, "What do I do now?".'

Which will prompt a third player to say: 'What a character Joe was, when he was here. He and Mick used to go a round together, and whatever Joe did, Mick would follow. If Joe bought a sports car, Mick would buy one. I remember following them down the road one day in my car, and I stopped behind them at traffic lights. All of a sudden, both doors of the cars in front of me opened, and Joe and Mick were out and sprinting for the wall on their respective sides. Then they dashed back, to get back into their cars before the lights had changed to green. There was a lorry driver next to me, and he was pissing himself watching 'em. They were two mad buggers.'

I remember right at the start of my career, at Manchester United, when there was the glamour of those European trips to far-away places, and Brian Kidd became noted as the greatest bargain hunter in the party. It's commonplace for Western tourists to bargain over the prices asked in the Eastern bazaars, where this is the expected thing, in any event, but 'Kiddo' maintained the habit even when we went shopping on the Continent. He would never be prepared to pay the asking price for anything – he would start to haggle, in the hope of getting some discount on his purchase.

He was a great mickey-taker, too. When we went on tour to Israel, we visited Jerusalem and the Wailing Wall. That night, we were back in our hotel in Tel Aviv, and sitting in the restaurant waiting to order a meal when

'Kiddo' walked in, but instead of coming to join us at the table, he walked straight over to the far wall of the restaurant, and began to do his impression of the action we had seen at the Wailing Wall. We really didn't know where to put ourselves.

It was 'Kiddo', too, who went for a stroll in the grounds of our hotel on the eve of the European Cup final, and decided he wanted to take a lily leaf from the pool there. So he lay down and got Francis Burns to keep a firm hold on his feet, so that he wouldn't overbalance and fall in. 'Burnsie' held him for a few seconds – then let go. 'Kiddo' ended up soaked, but he was more concerned about his money and that trainer Jack Crompton shouldn't discover he'd been in the pool. So he beat a hasty retreat to his room, there to dry not only himself, but the money on the radiator. But he had to scoop up the money and bundle it hastily into a drawer when Jack walked into the room.

Nobby Stiles, of course, was famous for his short-sightedness, and on my first European trip I wondered why the other players were leaving Nobby with a row of seats to himself in the aircraft. I took a seat close by him, and then I discovered why the 'regulars' left Nobby to his own devices when the drinks were served, for as he began to pour, a considerable amount missed his glass and went all over my new grey flannel trousers – and I couldn't get the stain out. I remember when we were in Greece, too, how someone else had vision trouble, as we were sitting round the swimming pool at the hotel. This time it wasn't Nobby, but a reporter who walked straight through a plate-glass window.

It was a standing joke among the players that you didn't need to ask for a menu when Nobby was around – you just asked for his tie, because that was where all the food was. And he could be absent-minded. Once, he took his wife and mother-in-law to the railway station, saw them off on the train, then went back to his car, felt in his pockets – and couldn't find his ignition key. So he hailed a taxi and went home, knowing he had a spare set of keys there. But he couldn't get into the house, so he went back in the taxi to where his car was standing. He got in the car, began searching for the keys again, looking to see if they might have fallen under the dashboard, felt a tap on the front of his nose . . . and discovered that they had been in the ignition all the time.

Sometimes you wonder about your team-mates – what they're really like, deep down inside. George Best, for instance. When United were spending a few days in Jersey, and out in front at the top of the First Division table. George was more than chirpy – over a drink one night, he began enthusing about it all, what it would be like to win the championship, and so on. He was quite carried away with the vision of success. Then relate the feelings he must have had a month later, when we had lost every game bar one, and things had fallen apart for him and the club, and perhaps the public might have had more understanding of his reactions.

Bobby Charlton was the introvert, quite the opposite of his brother, Jack. I was pally with Steve James, and when we were in Majorca on tour, Bobby came into the bar one night and joined us for a drink. It was then, for the first time, to my knowledge, that he let his hair down and began to show his true feelings about events and people, and I discerned that while he wasn't enamoured of George and his antics, he wasn't a faithful believer in everything Frank O'Farrell did, either. It was instructive in so far as there was Bobby, sipping a lager and expounding views in private that a newspaper might have paid a lot of money to publicise.

I was with Huddersfield when Bobby had his testimonial game at Old Trafford, and I received an invite to the slap-up function which followed at a Manchester hotel. Frank, I noticed, wasn't sitting at the top table, and it was clearly indicative of the way that things were developing. Frank, who had greeted me like a long-lost son in the foyer, got the bullet the following day. At that reception, I met John Aston, senior, who told me that, with hindsight, Frank would probably have kept me, and young Johnny Aston, at United, had he his time over again.

On one occasion, Denis Law introduced me to his best friend, Gordon Lowe, who had been a young player at Huddersfield with him. While Denis had moved on to bigger things, Gordon left Huddersfield for Bristol City, and never became what is popularly called a Soccer Star. But Denis never let the friendship lapse, and I found, too, that there can be sentiment or thoughtfulness in football, at times, when you least expect it.

More than once, Denis took me under his wing, and I shall always be grateful to him for those little acts of kindness, as he went out of his way to make me feel at home on social occasions. Gordon Lowe remembered me, too, for he visited me in hospital at Huddersfield, after I had been knocked out cold in two successive matches. The second time, I was really suffering from concussion, and when I awoke in a hospital bed I didn't know whether I was already married, or if I were due to get married in the very near future. The latter was the case, for my wedding day had been fixed for the following Monday, and I can see Henry Cockburn's young son now, asking his Dad if there would be a substitute for me at the wedding. Henry then was on the backroom staff at Huddersfield.

When I was at United – Manchester United – people often used to mistake me for goalkeeper Alex Stepney.

I used to go into a city restaurant for lunch, and the wait-ress there always used to greet me with: 'Hello, Alex luv, how are you today!' I never corrected her, and she went blissfully on her way thinking she'd been chatting to Alex Stepney. But one day, when I took Lynn, my wife, into the restaurant, the game was up, for when the wait-ress said, 'Hello, Alex luv,' Lynn – not knowing what had gone before – smiled and said: 'His name's Alan – and it's Gowling, not Stepney.'

In my early days at Newcastle, it was Paddy Howard with whom people got me confused. They would stop me in the street and address me at 'Pat', thinking they were talking to the man who played at centre-back for New-castle. And I became involved in another case of mistaken identity during a game at Queen's Park Rangers, after I had gone off injured and taken an early bath and got changed. When Geoff Nulty was hurt later, I left the bench and helped him off the field and along to the treatment room – where the Rangers doctor thought I was the Newcastle trainer.

He took a look at Geoff, then began to give me instruc-tions. 'Keep him still . . . he'll be all right . . . but you'll have to see that he rests up for two or three days.' When I got back to the bench, I was feeling highly amused at having been taken for the trainer . . . but the party wasn't quite over, because as the game ended, and I got up to go back to the dressing-room, a fellow grabbed my arm and told me the Press would like to talk to me. Only this time, they thought I was Richard Dinnis, who had taken charge of the team after Gordon Lee's departure for Everton.

Gordon Lee signed two of his former Blackburn players for Newcastle: goalkeeper Roger Jones and utility player Graham Oates. Graham is a big lad, a gentle giant of a man. We call him 'Sam'. He's self-effacing, and normally

you wouldn't expect him to say 'boo' to a goose. I'd never
known him lose his temper, although he can obviously
look after himself, but when we were on tour in Majorca,
he showed everyone that he wasn't going to be messed about.

'Sam', Mickey Burns, Roger Jones and myself were playing table-tennis, and suddenly, water began to fall from
the balcony just above. Then there was another bucketful . . . and the third bucketful went all over 'Sam'. He
took two steps back, looked up at the balcony, and saw
Malcolm Macdonald and goalkeeper Mike Mahoney there,
killing themselves with laughter. 'Sam' didn't waste words.
'You do that again, and I'll be up there and throw the
pair of you over the balcony.' He didn't regard himself as
one of the glamour boys at the club, but in that brief
moment he impressed himself on all the lads who saw the
incident. No more water came down from the balcony.

'Sam' had a brush with a spectator during his days as
a player at Bradford. The spectator was either very brave,
or just daft. As the players were leaving the field, after
the game, 'Sam' heard the fellow call out: 'Oates, you're
effing useless!' Without ado, 'Sam' was over the wall and
on to the terraces – luckily for the spectator, the manager
and another player managed to restrain 'Sam'.

When I was at Huddersfield, the fans got on to me one
day, because I was having a bad game. I thought I was
being treated unfairly, because my overall record wasn't
bad, and I'd scored a few goals for the club. So I decided
to answer the criticisms in my own way, and I came out
and said that they were unfair, and that in future I would
decline to attend any more functions in the area, until
the criticisms stopped. People who understood my aggra-
vation pointed out to me that the barracking was coming
from a minority of supporters so, having made my own
point, and seen it sink home, I decided not to press it.

It was at Huddersfield that The Phantom used to strike. It became the accepted thing that when you were staying overnight for an away match, you never left your room key with reception, and you made sure that when you left your room, you hid your toilet bag and checked that the room door was securely locked. If you made either of those two mistakes, you could be sure you'd pay for it, because when you returned to your room, you would find all the bristles on your toothbrush had been burned, your toothpaste tube punctured in about 20 places, and boot polish on your shaving brush. Plus the message: 'The Phantom strikes again.' We never did find out the identity of The Phantom, either.

Huddersfield were playing at Bristol, and the night before we met City we stayed in an hotel – that was before the purse strings had to be tightened at Leeds-road – and around two o'clock in the morning, the fire alarm went off. It was the first time I'd ever been in such a situation, and I wasn't quite sure what to do – so I lay there, waiting for something to happen.

Then I got up, and opened the door, to see other players' heads emerging from the other bedroom doors along the corridor. We decided there was no need to panic, and went back inside our rooms. But with the alarm still clanging away five minutes later, I decided not to risk being a dead hero (or idiot), so I packed my case and, still in my pyjamas, went down the fire exit and finished up in the hotel lobby.

There were about 30 other guests there, too, all in their night attire, but none of the Huddersfield players had put in an appearance. I felt a bit foolish when I learned that a sprinkler had gone off by accident, and that it was a false alarm, although, to be on the safe side, the fire brigade had been summoned.

Footballers are noted for their ability to consume a meal

in quick time, and at Newcastle United there is a Noshers' League. Alan Kennedy, Geoff Nulty and myself are leading lights, but Mike Mahoney is the undisputed No. 1 nosher. When Geoff broke his jaw, it was agony for him, because he could take only liquids, since the jaw was wired and he could barely move his mouth.

One day, however, he reckoned he was getting along a bit better – he could just manage to get a bit of solid food through the gap in his teeth. But the next time he went back to hospital for a check-up on the jaw, they put a stop to that, by tightening the frame and so effectively plugging the gap between his top and bottom teeth. That put him out of the running in the Noshers' League for another six weeks.

As the champion, Mike Mahoney has a reputation to uphold, and you'll see him scorch through bread rolls, soup, and the main course – then, shortly afterwards, he'll announce that he's feeling hungry, and be ready to nosh again. When we were in Majorca, Geoff Nulty didn't miss a meal in the hotel, and despite the Spanish-style cooking, he ate everything that was offered. We awarded him an extra mark in the Noshers' League for that . . . Mickey Burns and myself picked at our food mostly, then went out and spent most of our money on food we were more accustomed to eating at home. Of course, it had to include chips.

Newcastle's players have a golf competition too – they call it the Magpie Masters' Trophy. Shortly after Graham Oates arrived at St James's Park, we held the first Magpie Masters event of the season, and when he told us he played off a handicap of 24, we felt charitably disposed towards this newcomer. We played a round in the morning, and he found himself having five shots knocked off his handicap. We went out again in the afternoon, and after he had won, we knocked another four shots off his handicap.

But 'Sam' still stoutly maintained that he was a 24-handicap golfer. And he's still claiming this.

The story about the Irishman which I mentioned earlier was fictitious, of course. The story about the Irishman – Tommy Cassidy by name – at Newcastle United is true. We played a mid-week match in London, and travelled back to Newcastle by train, arriving home very late. All the players' boots were packed in a big bag, and when we reported for training on the Friday morning, we were somewhat surprised to find that the trainer wasn't already there. It was getting on for 11 o'clock then, so we asked what was going on. It seem that nobody could find the bag with the boots in it.

It was thought the boot bag had been left on the train, or was lying around somewhere at the station, waiting to be claimed. So the trainer had gone down to the railway station, to see if he could locate the boots. Suddenly, Tommy Cassidy vanished. He went out to the car park, unlocked the boot of his car . . . and produced the missing boot bag, which he'd stuck in the car boot for safety, when we'd returned from London.

Tommy Craig, who is a Scottish internationl player, is rightly proud of his country, despite all the jokes people make about Scots. But he had an unhappy experience when we were in Majorca. We used to drop into a little bar which was owned by a Scot, and the players spent quite a few bob in that bar, each evening. Tommy would tell us, night after night, that the bar owner would reciprocate, before we departed for home, but we showed him that we were sceptical. On the last night, we still hadn't had a drink 'on the house', but Tommy stuck to his guns, and when the bar owner asked us when we were returning home, and we told him it was our last evening in Majorca, Tommy was ready to say: 'There, what did I tell you?'

But all we got from the bar owner was: 'Thanks very much for your custom, lads . . . good-bye.'

Tommy's reputation as a racing tipster didn't get much of a boost, either, when we entered a competition run by a national newspaper for players of certain clubs. The idea was that each club received £100, and the players – or a particular player – would use the cash to put on horses selected by him, in the hope that over a period of time you would show a profit.

The clubs were in competition – I think Liverpool and Manchester United were among the entries – and Tommy was the man who did our tipping. Anything over the £100 was yours to keep, and the eventual champions received a crate of champagne. We lost the £100, Tommy lost his reputation as a tipster, and Villa sank the champagne.

Footballers are great practical jokers, and Alan Kennedy, another of the Newcastle players, was always having his leg pulled about the telephone calls he received from a girl friend – or was it girl friends? – Every time the phone rings at the training ground, we yell for Alan and tell him it's 'Shirley' on the line. The odds are that it's a sports reporter wanting to talk to one of the other players.

At Chelsea, they have a phone in the visitors' dressing-room, and when we were playing at Stamford Bridge one day, we were all changed into our strip and set to go out for the pre-match kickabout when one of the players picked up the phone, spoke a few words, then called Alan back. 'It's for you – it's Shirley,' he said. Alan was quick to get to the phone, and I don't know what he would have said if his girl friend had been at the other end of the line . . . but as soon as he spoke, he realised there was no one there. It had been another leg-pull.

Stewart Barrowclough 'nutmegs' people, all the time.

He'll do it in warm-up sessions, when you're doing exercises, and he'll try to 'nutmeg' people without the ball, in certain situations. But he was 'nutmegged' himself when we were playing a derby game against Sunderland at Roker Park. Tickets for these matches are precious, of course, and although the players get a small allocation, they could always use more tickets. Before the game, when we were in the dressing-room, the tickets were distributed among the players, who then nipped out and passed them on to their friends and relatives.

Richard Dinnis 'nutmegged' Stewart, when he took from his pocket two tickets for the previous game, against Birmingham. Stewart had already been out to distribute his ticket allocation, and on his return to the dressing-room, Richard said he could have these two tickets. So Stewart went out again, and left them with the doorman, to give to friends.

Five minutes later, the doorman was in the dressing-room, pointing out that Stewart had deposited two tickets for the Birmingham match with him. Unabashed, Stewart told us that he'd been trying to 'nutmeg' the people for whom he'd left the tickets.

Players are sometimes superstitious. When we were travelling to Leeds for the second replay of our FA Cup-tie against Bolton, and our coach became jammed in traffic, so that we were pushed for time, and arrived at the Elland-road ground only 40 minutes before the kick-off, you might have thought the Newcastle players would have been feeling on tenterhooks and even a bit upset. Yet the opposite was the case.

We felt confident that it was going to be our night BECAUSE there'd been a bit of a 'cock-up' on the way to the game. It seems that every time we get involved in a mixed-up situation, things turn out for the best. We've had some good results at Loftus-road against Queen's Park Rangers, and we've had some 'cock-ups' when we've played there, too, so that makes Loftus-road one of our favourite grounds. We arrived for a League Cup-tie there (we won, and went to Wembley), to find that there had been a bit of a mix-up about playing kit, as a result of which Stewart Barrowclough looked like Wee Willie Winkie as he was getting into a shirt that was miles too big for him.

Another time, we arrived almost before the gates had been opened. That day, we'd expected a lot of traffic, and we'd had a smooth run, so instead of arriving at Loftus-road an hour before kick-off time, we were there to welcome the first customers through the turnstiles. Then, more recently, we went to play Rangers – and forgot the shin-pads. But again, we won. And we arrived at St Andrew's for a game against Birmingham almost an hour and a half before kick-off time . . . and won that match. No wonder we say: 'Let's have a cock-up before the game, and we're sure to win!'

From the players' point of view, there are five main facets which are important: skill, confidence, fitness, character and . . . luck. There is no particular order of importance for these themes, because each player may see the situation in a different light, placing the emphasis on skill, confidence, fitness or character, as the primary factor. But luck is the exception – it's the intangible factor that has its own place in the world of the professional footballer.

'Without luck, the rest wouldn't work. Luck is the vital element.'

'Lucky breaks make all the difference. I would never have got started in this game, but for a stroke of good luck.'

Or (in a different context): 'I don't believe in luck . . .

you make your own luck. Footballers are always talking about the breaks having gone against them, but that's just looking for an excuse."

Listening to the conversation of professional footballers off the field, and their expletives on it, you cannot fail to notice the emphasis which is placed on that four-letter word, 'luck'.

'We didn't get the run of the ball today' . . . 'They're getting all the breaks' . . . 'Keep on plugging away, and you'll get the breaks' . . . these are phrases commonly heard (with an expletive or two thrown in) during half-time or after a game. On the field, during the match itself, there's little time for conversation, although a certain former Manchester United player was once heard talking to a team-mate about the film he was going to see that night. But on the field, verbal exchanges are short and common – and not usually so sweet. 'You lucky bugger' . . . 'You lucky bastard' . . . these are commonly exchanged, among the effing and the blinding. That's the language of a hard, physical game.

It has often been said by people in the game that football is a game of luck, even though skill, fitness, confidence and character are essential elements. There's luck as an excuse for having lost, or miscued a pass ('the ball bobbled as I hit it'); luck as an explanation for something which has happened when it didn't seem possible; and luck as a superstition.

Luck as an explanation? – Yes . . . for example, why a perfectly-struck ball hits a post and rebounds on to the field of play, or why a ball seemingly going wide of the post strikes a defender and goes into the goal. Logically, we know why these things have happened, because they're visible to us; but the footballer has to know more than what he's seen. He wants to know why, having hit the defender, the bloody ball didn't go harmlessly wide, or back into play. He's seeking a deeper explanation of what was so apparent.

I've never yet met a footballer who claimed to be an Anzanda (most players would ask, 'An – effing – who?), but if a footballer were an Anzanda, he might well turn to witchcraft for his answer and consult the poison oracle. As one writer pointed out: 'The concept of witchcraft... provides them with a natural philosophy by which relations between men and unfortunate events are explained, and a ready and stereotyped means of reacting to such events.' In a similar way, the footballer, looking for the casual explanation, chooses to use luck as the answer to the problem. If he were religious, he might say it was 'the will of God'; but he tends to be agnostic, and so he simply uses luck as the explanation.

Luck, of course, can be used to explain good fortune, as well as bad. Footballers recognise that they have lucky breaks, as well as unlucky breaks. But they don't acknowledge this quite so readily.

They would rather put the element of good luck down to their own good play, although, in their sober moments, they will concede that 'everything went for us today.'

They will often explain their own careers in the same way. They realise that to get to the top in the game necessitates a considerable degree of luck, at some stage in their career. In my own case, I have to thank some lucky star for the fact that, at a moment when my career appeared to be in almost total eclipse, I was given the chance to stride back straight into the First Division. The fact that I believed I had something still to offer at the highest level in the game was something; but I needed that intangible element called 'luck' to get my chance of proving it.

10   The Man in the Middle

I was invited to Roker Park – not to sign for Sunderland, but to talk to a meeting of North-East League referees and linesmen. I was astounded to learn that, although such invitations had been issued before, I was the first player who had accepted this chance to get together with the men who play such an important part in the game. And despite the smirks which may follow that statement, I maintain that the referee IS a vital cog in the machinery of professional football.

There are good referees and there are bad ones. From the players' point of view, the good referee is the man who recognises that the football pitch is the equivalent of the shop floor at an engineering works, which means that he is not too concerned with the 'industrial language' which is used by players during a game. The good referee knows that because players become so involved during a game, they can easily lose their heads in the heat of the moment, and they give vent to their feelings by using 'industrial language.' Sometimes it's directed at opponents, sometimes against a referee's decision, sometimes, even, against themselves. The referee who makes allowances is very much appreciated by the players, take it from me.

A good referee also has the ability to spot and to get on top of the professional fouls, early in the game. There are the sly kicks, the trips and niggling nudges, and the tackles which, while not dangerous, are calculated to in-timidate. Players soon sense if a referee is going to take a grip, or let things slide. I can think of a referee who handled a game when Newcastle were playing away, and a few brief words from him showed the players that he wasn't going to get a grip on things, for he warned one player: 'Go over the top again, and you're off.'

That remark incensed us, because the referee had ob-viously seen the over-the-top tackle, and such a tackle is the cardinal sin in football. It can maim a player, and cut short his career. A badly-broken leg can result from an over-the-top tackle. In that match, the referee didn't even book the offender, and this upset the Newcastle players. From then on, things began to get rather heated, and niggling fouls became the order of the day. Yet still no one was booked.

I can think of another occasion, during my days at Huddersfield, where a team came to Leeds-road and began kicking early on. The referee soon showed he knew what was happening, and he finished up by sending off two of the visiting players, for having committed dangerous fouls. In my book, that referee did his job courageously, and he was right. I admired the referee's courage because from experience I know that a lot of referees will not give players marching orders for tackles which could have broken an opponent's leg. I believe a referee has to take strong action, when this sort of thing happens.

If a referee is seen to be avoiding his responsibilty, it can create many problems for him during the rest of the game, because the players begin to take advantage of his laxness, and they end up by taking matters into their own hands, and dispensing their own brand of justice upon the offenders. Further, a referee can irritate players if he is constantly finger-wagging, calling a man over and giving him a public lecture; the quiet word can be much more effective. So what I am saying is that footballers want to be treated like men, and not like kids.

I thought Gordon Hill was a tremendous referee, although I suspect that he wasn't as popular with authority as he was with players. If you made a good tackle, or put in a good shot, two or three seconds later, as he was running past you, Gordon would say, 'Good effort', or 'Well done.' At the same time, if you gave a heated reply on the spur of the moment to one of his decisions, he would let you know in no uncertain terms what he thought of your reaction, without getting the book out.

All football teams strive for consistency, and all players agree that consistency is what is required in refereeing. But we don't always get it. Nothing annoys players more than to see a referee give one decision for an incident and then, a few minutes later, fail to give a repeat decision for a similiar incident. Players want a consistent approach – and they would rather a referee made two bad decisions, providing they're the same, than give one bad decision and no decision at all, shortly afterwards. Footballers always appreciate the referee who can let the insignificant things pass, but who doesn't dally when a tough line needs to be taken.

As a striker, I know that a lot goes on inside the box – from both sides. Sometimes referees miss it; sometimes, I'm sure, a ref hesitates to take action because it means a penalty. There was some argument when Liverpool and Everton replayed an FA Cup semi-final at Maine-road in the spring of 1977, and Everton defender Micky Pejic was ruled to have committed an offence which brought Liverpool a penalty. As the ball came in, Pejic appeared to me to push a player away, and I thought that referee Clive Thomas did tremendously well in spotting what had happened, and in awarding Liverpool a penalty. It was a brave decision, in such a vital match.

At one time, Clive had a reputation for booking players left, right and centre, especially after the disciplinary clamp-down of a few seasons ago. He really went by the book. But he has turned over a new leaf, and in games he has handled involving Newcastle during the past couple of seasons or so, I have admired him more and more. We had Clive Thomas in a game at Birmingham, and he was excellent. The pitch was hard and bumpy, and the ball didn't run true. He realised conditions were difficult for the players, and that this meant there would be more physical contact than usual, and he applied the rules not only fairly, but with common sense. Almost on the final whistle, Newcastle got a winning goal, and as we were running back to the centre circle, Clive observed: 'I think you've just about deserved it.' It showed a complete change in character for Clive . . . a touch of the Gordon Hill. And we appreciated it.

Pat Partridge, Tony Morrissey and Colin Seel are referees who, for my money, know their business, too. We don't see a lot of Pat, as he is based in the North-East, but on the occasions when he has handled a game in which I've been playing, I've found him fair, and prepared to accept the rough-and-tumble of the game. He'll overlook a player's instant verbal reaction.

Some referees take this instant reaction as a personal slight upon themselves, although it is right for a referee to get tough with a persistent complainer. The good referee, however, disappears into the game, while at the same time letting the players know he is there, and keeping a watchful eye on proceedings.

My team-mate, Mickey Burns, got marching orders in a match which we lost, 3–2. We had scored first, then our opponents equalised, and the next goal came from a very dubious penalty which the referee awarded to them, after one of their forwards, in our view, had blatantly dived in the area. Once the award had been given, we took up various positions as we waited for the spot-kick to be taken, and it was during this lull that Mickey said to an opposing player: 'That was a f . . .ing useless decision.' The referee was 10 yards away, but he must have thought Mickey was talking to him, and he promptly booked my team-mate, and sent him off. Mickey couldn't believe it, but he had to walk. Newcastle sent in a report on the incident, and although normally a one-match suspension would have followed, in this case no action was taken, so obviously the powers-that-be felt he had been dealt with severely enough, by being sent off.

I have a lot of respect for Jack Taylor, who has just retired from the League list, but there was one occasion when my opinion of him was less than 100 per cent. I was playing for Manchester United against West Ham, and the ball was played into our penalty area. It was an innocent enough ball, with no danger to us, and I turned to chest the ball down. Possibly my action was deceptive, and certainly Jack Taylor must have thought I had used my arm to control the ball, for he gave a penalty. As it happened, the ground was muddy, and we were playing in white shirts . . . and I was able to turn and show Jack the perfect imprint of the ball on my chest. But he had already given the penalty.

In another match, when I was playing for Huddersfield against Aldershot during my Third Division days, the centre-half and I were having a real ding-dong battle, especially when we went up together for the ball in the air. But every time we went up, the referee would come across and warn us about our play, and it got to the stage where he booked both of us for illegal challenges. Frankly, we were both puzzled and a bit upset, for we had been enjoying the cut-and-thrust of this physical combat, and from then on we were all too conscious of the bookings and the fact that the next step could be marching orders. In those circumstances, you tend to lose your concentration on the game, because you're worrying about the referee's reactions.

That was the third booking of my career – the first came when I was playing for Manchester United, and it was for alleged time-wasting at a throw-in, when we met Southampton in an FA Cup replay at Old Trafford. I went to take the throw, and I was trying to find a team-mate who was unmarked. You don't just chuck the ball straight into space, or to an opponent. The next thing that happened was that George Best came over and told me to leave the ball for him to take the throw. I did as George said, and found myself being booked. I was very upset by what I considered an unfair booking.

My second booking came when I committed a foul against Frank Spraggon, who was then playing at full-back for Middlesbrough. He was going upfield on a flank sortie, and moving like an express train, as I chased after him. I saw that he was going to cross the ball, so I tried to slide-tackle him, and brought him down just as he had knocked the ball a yard or two further on. It was a late tackle, and I caught Frank fairly heavily, as we were both going at speed. I think the tackle looked worse than it was, but I had no complaints about the booking.

My third booking was in the game against Aldershot, and my fourth booking came when Newcastle played Bristol City at Ashton Gate, at a time when City were fighting desperately to stay in the First Division. From the start, it was a very physical game, and I soon began to take some stick from more than one opponent. In the end, I began to feel annoyed at what I considered was lack of protection from the referee. From the opening minutes, there had been a visible sign, for an opponent had come down my leg with his boot, leaving a gaping hole in my stocking. No action had been taken over this foul, though. I was caught once or twice again after that, and – completely out of character – I was finally goaded into taking my own action, to even the score. The ball was played, and I tried to catch ball and opponent together. I mistimed my tackle, and caught the player, although it wasn't an over-the-top tackle. So my name went into the book.

I'll admit to being one of the biggest moaners in the game – but I moan to myself, and not at other people. If an opponent puts one across me or gets away with something, I'll mutter to myself, 'You lucky bastard . . .', or if I miss narrowly with a shot or a header, I'll tell myself, 'Bloody hard luck . . .' And if I'm complaining about a referee's decision, I try to keep the complaint to myself. That's not to say I never question a referee's decision to his face, and there is no doubt that the man in the middle often comes in for some stick from players. He's the human factor, the visible target, the tangible element when things have gone against them. The fact that he's human, and can be seen to perpetrate mistakes, gives a player the perfect alibi for his own error, on occasion.

When I met the North-East referees, at the invitation of their president, Pat Partridge, I sensed that there was a tremendous spirit of camaraderie among them, and although there were between 30 and 40 of them, they made me feel welcome. I had no feeling of having entered the lions' den.

I didn't pull any punches when I addressed them,

although I tried to be objective, and they listened to me
with apparent interest. I told them what I strongly believe
– that there should be much more communication between
players and referees. When you're out on the park, and
running around for 90 minutes, the game demands co-
operation between players and referees, even though we
have different attitudes and different jobs to do. I put it
to the referees that they are not encouraged to socialise
with players after a game, but that I felt it could do a
great deal of good if players and referees could join together for an after-match drink. At such a time, a player
could reasonably ask a referee to explain a decision during
the game, and although there might be argument, and
even heated opposing viewpoints, there would be much
more good come out of such face-to-face discussions, because I am convinced that each side would achieve a far
greater understanding of the other's problems. The idea
seemed to go down quite well.

When I had given my side of the picture, the referees
got the chance to ask questions and present their case. I
had to concede, for instance, that players had a moral
obligation to put a stop to over-the-top tackling, but I
countered that the referee was the man who had the direct
authority to clamp down, by issuing marching orders for
the first deliberate offence of this nature in a game. The
referees didn't think that players, generally speaking,
knew the rules of the game as they should do, and I feel
myself that young footballers should be made aware of the
laws, and their application, and that coaches could test
them on their knowledge.

Another point was that I advocated more ex-professional
referees. That doesn't mean I want to see full-time professional referees. I accept that the men doing the job at
present are dedicated, by and large. They don't take up

reffing because they are in the game for the money.

There are a handful of referees who did kick off as would-be professional footballers. Some of them had their careers cut short by injury, and others dropped out of the professional scene for other reasons. The referees felt that men who had been players might not be attracted by the match fees for officials, and I made the point that when you've played the game as a professional until you're in your middle 30's, it doesn't leave much scope for you to get to the top as a referee.

Not all former players would make good referees, either, in the same way that a star footballer doesn't necessarily make a top manager. As for the money side of it, only those former players who were dedicated enough would be ready – and acceptable – to become referees when they had hung up their playing boots. The match fee must be incidental: it's the involvement that matters.

11 The Hard Men

Over the years I've learned to live with the fact that people expect you to get goals week after week, if you're labelled a striker. As a newcomer to League football, I soon experienced the attentions of defenders who, to put it mildly, tried to impose themselves on me. There was intimidation, both physical and verbal, at times. 'Whack him in the first few minutes, and let him know you're the boss' seemed to be the motto of some of my opponents.

Indeed, my first experience of what it was going to be like making my way in top-class football came when I was playing for Manchester United's reserve team, and I was in direct opposition to a centre-half who had won England honours. In no way did he have a reputation for being a dirty player, but he was a down-to-earth, dyed-in-the-wool professional. After I had managed to win the ball a few times, I duly received the warning: 'I'm going to have you!'

I ignored this danger signal, but later in the game, we both went for a high ball and as we fell together, my opponent came down the back of my leg with his boot. The injury put me out of action for a couple of weeks, and that first lesson taught me about one of the 'professional' fouls in football, for I've seen that trick done often enough, since that day.

Another centre-half who found the going hard against me unceremoniously brought me to earth several times in the first quarter of an hour of a match, and duly collected a booking for his attentions to me. And in fairness to opponents, I have to admit that I tend to be a bit robust myself, for I never shirk a challenge, and I'm ready to do my share of the knocking about. My old Manchester United team-mate, David Sadler, will recall a practice match in which he was marking me. He had just returned from injury, after having broken a cheek bone, and as the pair of us went for a bouncing ball inside the six-yard box, I put in my usual, 100 per cent challenge. David took the full brunt of it. He didn't take too kindly to the treatment, either, and later on he sorted me out, when he went into a tackle and whacked me one. So we finished up even . . . and having a healthy, mutual respect.

When a player comes down the back of your calf with his studs, to the Achilles tendon, it's often impossible for the referee to spot that this was a deliberate foul, for both striker and defender are going for the ball together, and each player usually ends up off balance. It's when you're coming down that the crafty defender can catch you, and you find that, at best, you've got a cut around the ankles. At worst, it can mean ligament trouble which puts you on the sidelines for two or three weeks. In that sort of situation, once you've experienced the treatment, you learn pretty quickly how to survive.

My attitude is that if an opponent is going to beat me, he's going to have to show thousands of spectators – and Alan Gowling – that he's the better player. And the more he tries to clobber me, the more he'll have to try, in terms of footballing ability, because I'll keep coming back and challenging. One of the strong points of my game is my temperament: I always consciously attempt to remain unruffled. And this can be disconcerting to an opponent.

Referees are constantly criticised for their failure to stamp out (or inability to spot) dirty play. Injuries are something the player must live with, from match to match – he accepts that a particular game might be his last, although he doesn't dwell on this. There are the hard men in football, and there are the dirty players. The two are not necessarily the same. The hard men rely on strength and aggression, as well as skill; they play the game forcefully, to overcome opponents. The term 'hard men' is used more of defenders, because it's their job to stifle the skill of forwards in the best way they think fit.

They play the game in a hard manner, appearing to be immune to the pain of physical clashes. Their role is to 'destroy' opponents, to stop the opponents' creative play and win the ball from them to start their own attack. At times, they are seen to take their role as 'destroyers' literally, and on occasion they may scythe down an opponent. But you have to remember that the game is played at speed, and that to make a fair tackle requires the skill of timing and anticipation. Movement and deceptive play inevitably mean that players are sometimes going to get kicked, and that tackles will not always be fair.

The hard man generally makes strong, fair tackles, capitalising on the skill he possesses, but occasionally he is deceived or misreads a situation to which he has already committed himself with a strong, physical challenge. Committed, and having no fear of the physical clash, he goes on to whack his opponent. The dirty player, as I have said, isn't necessarily the hard man. Anyone can be a dirty player – a defender, a midfield man or a forward. Dirty play, quite simply, is deliberately dangerous play which might bring injury to an opponent and the cardinal sin, as I have mentioned elsewhere, is going over the top – going over the ball in a tackling situation, and kicking the op-

E

ponent's leg. Since serious injury can result, players are particularly maddened by it.

The dirty players are well-enough known in the game. Anyone can commit a foul, but the regular offenders are acknowledged among the players. They are differentiated, also, by degrees from the 'niggling' player, the man who is always ankle-tapping, kicking the back of the heels, or pulling an opponent's shirt. The 'niggler' isn't out to deliberately injure an opponent, but to upset him, to make him lose concentration on the ball and during the game. The 'niggler' can present such a problem that after the opponent has been subjected to his attentions several times, his temper begins to boil, and although he tries to keep it bottled up, just one more bit of ankle-tapping or shirt-pulling can produce the explosion, and a violent reaction. And retaliation can then get the previously innocent party in trouble.

I have scanned quickly through the First Division clubs, and I must say that it is difficult to find many players who can be classified in the dirty brigade. They do not reach double figures. But there are nine men who, in my opinion, can go over the top without scruple, when the mood suits them. Four are defenders, three are midfield men, one plays in midfield or up front, and the last is an out-and-out striker. Five of them have won caps.

Two of the most skilled forwards of yesteryear – neither of them a giant – could be rated as among the most experienced over-the-top players in the game. So the dirty player, as I've said, doesn't have to be a defender. A forward ready to go over the top can have the ball at his feet, pretend to be about to lose control, and entice a defender to commit himself to the tackle. The forward will then go over the top. Alternatively, you can wait for an opponent to receive the ball and momentarily lose control of it, and you go into the tackle and over the top. The clever ones can go over the top with the ball at their own feet. And once this business starts during a game, it becomes a vicious circle, for if the referee fails to take action, the victims seek to exact their own form of retribution.

I have already mentioned earlier my own initiation into the hard world of professional football, where an international centre-half tried to cut me down to size. I don't intend to name the dirty players I have mentioned, for obvious reasons. But I will say that one of them taught me always to beware, while one of the cleanest players in the game – Bobby Charlton – taught me how to escape such ungentlemanly attentions.

It was an end-of-season match at Old Trafford, and there was nothing at stake for either side, when I was made painfully aware of what can happen when a guy goes over the top. I'd gone on as substitute for the last few minutes of the match, and I was still comparatively wet behind the ears, so far as the world of the professionals was concerned. I received the ball with my back to an opposing defender, although he wasn't tight-marking me, and as I turned, he went in, not to play the ball, but to go over the top. He clouted me on the knee. So I got away without a serious injury, and perhaps I had Bobby Charlton to thank in some measure for that.

I used to watch Bobby, and I had noticed that he was very good at getting both feet off the ground. In my early days, I got a lot of ankle injuries because I was caught with one foot on the ground, so I was getting hammered while all my weight was on that foot, and a whack meant that it was taking all the strain. Bobby was a past-master at getting both feet off the ground at the moment he was hit, and so he rode the force of the tackle and just fell. He might have a bruise to show for it, but that was better than damaged ligaments. In that particular match, as I turned I saw from the corner of my eye that the defender was going for me, and I did a Bobby Charlton, lifting both feet from the ground . . . so I got away with a bruised knee.

Let me say here that from experience, I found that players in the lower divisions were not more prone to go over the top than those in the First Division, and that with experience, you can find you're waiting for someone to go over the top at you. In my book, you cannot differentiate with an over-the-top tackle – every single one is as bad as the other, and the penalty for each should be marching orders.

So now I come to the hard men in the game, and names that immediately spring to mind are Tommy Smith, Mike Doyle, Denis Smith, Allan Hunter, Gordon McQueen, David Webb, Frank McLintock, Dave Watson, Chris Nicholl, Mike Lyons, Roger Kenyon, John Wile, Stuart Boam and Micky Pejic. Not one of these players needs to feel insulted because he is on my list – I have every admiration for the way they all use their strength, as well as their skill. They are physically hard; but they go in with the intention of winning the ball fairly, and when they do whack you, you have to accept it as one of the occupational hazards of the game.

Allan Hunter is hard, but he has a lot more skill than many people give him credit for; David Webb, a great character, is also a great professional; Frank McLintock's slim frame belies the strength in him, and I can only say that now he's a manager, I'll miss him as a direct opponent. When I played against Frank, I knew that if the ball was there, and you were on the other end of it, he'd let you know he was around, too, with a tackle. All these

players I have named know that when I'm around, I'm
not going to deliberately kick them, although I'll try
physical conclusions with them. So we know where we
stand.

I know that if I've got the ball, and one of these guys
tackles me, I'll feel it from the top of my head to the tips
of my toes . . . and I'm happy to accept the conditions
under which we compete. Tommy Smith commands my
utmost respect, and I will admit that only once during
our encounters have I got the better of the argument, when
we have clashed head-on. That was in a game at Anfield,
when the ball was played wide, and we both went challenging for possession. I managed to get there first, and I got
above Tommy as he was coming in at full steam. He
caught me – but it was Tommy who ended up on the deck,
while I walked away, still standing on my own two feet . . .
but still jarred in every bone in my body by the crunching
physical contact we had made. A minute later, with blood
still pouring down his face, Tommy was playing on.

I know, before every game, that a defender is going to
try conclusions with me at the earliest possible moment, to
let me know he's there. People say I don't give as good as
I get, but my style is to show that I can take it, and to keep
coming back for more, instead of getting ruffled and re-
taliating. That way, I reckon, I set a defender more problems. In time, I hope he'll become just a little bit
discouraged . . .

Mike Doyle and I used to train together, when we
played for the Stockport Boys team, but later we went our
separate ways, and the next time we met up it was in
front of a crowd of 60,000 people, in a Manchester derby
game. Mike was playing for City, I was in the United
side. He was a professional by then, while I was still an
amateur, but we both played without giving or expecting

to receive quarter. I finished that match with a strained calf muscle (not attributable to Mike), and he was claiming that City had scored a moral victory over United. He was then, and still is, a tremendous competitor.

He has had his brushes with referees, but I would never object to going into action against him, although there are times when, as Richard Dinnis said, Mike seems to think he's the referee, as well as one of the combatants! Richard felt strongly enough about it to say his piece when we were due to play Manchester City as they were chasing Liverpool for the League championship in season 1976–77. Richard thought that Mike was 'exceeding his powers' during the Manchester City-Arsenal game the previous Saturday. 'He was consistently chattering away to the referee, John Hunting, throughout an extremely physical game, and in my book that sort of thing is just not on.'

Richard conceded that Mike is 'a great player', and stressed that he wasn't picking on the City skipper. 'It's going on all the time, and to me it's nothing but gamesmanship. My players and I will be quite happy to abide by the referee's decisions tomorrow night. Doyle will give us enough problems with his ability alone.'

I think that Mike and I have a healthy enough respect for each other, and I recognise that when you are going for the League title, there is a great deal at stake, and the tensions run high. So perhaps I wouldn't criticise Mike Doyle so severely. And so far as the playing side is concerned, he comes into the 'hard man' category . . . but NOT the 'dirty' player class.

Mike's England and Manchester City team-mate, Dave Watson, is very much a marker who wants to pick up an opponent and dominate him physically. He also has a very unemotional appearance during a game – perhaps cold is a better word. You will go for the ball with Dave, meet each other head-on, and endure a bone-shuddering few seconds as you clash. But Dave will pick himself up or walk away without showing the slightest sign that he has felt the impact. I must say I've enjoyed our clashes, giving and taking knocks, and while I've never been able to fathom out Dave's feelings, I've noticed that other defenders usually seem to have a little smirk when they've put one across me.

Dave gives you the impression that he's utterly nerveless. Maybe it's all part of the act; maybe he genuinely doesn't get emotionally disturbed, either before or during a match. I get less keyed up now than I used to do, although I still maintain the same concentration. You can get yourself worked up so much that when you go on the field, you can do nothing right – this happened to me on my return to Old Trafford with Newcastle, and I was so determined to show the fans there that I still measured up to the demands of the top flight. I was keyed up to such a pitch that I couldn't shake off the nerves, and the result was that I couldn't seem to put a foot right during the whole of the 90 minutes. Not surprisingly, I took a bit of stick from the Old Trafford faithful, while no doubt the Manchester United players were quite happy to see that I was having a stinker.

Apart from Dave Watson and Mike Doyle, players who show no apparent nerves are Norman Hunter and Paul Madeley, while in my Old Trafford days I often used to look at Denis Law and George Best before a game, and wonder what they were really feeling – if anything. I found it much harder to get the odd butterfly during my days in the lower divisions – that was when I needed to concentrate on getting into the right frame of mind.

Go out at Anfield or Old Trafford, and the crowd generates atmosphere and sets the adrenalin flowing. But when you sat in the dressing-room at Huddersfield or some other ground in the lower divisions, and tried to work up an intense enthusiasm for playing in front of maybe 5,000 people, you had hard work to motivate yourself. It's not that way at Newcastle – you arrive at the ground, and as you get out of your car you are surrounded by the Geordie fanatics, wearing their black-and-white scarves, and you get caught up in the thrill of it all straight away. They'll ask you how many goals you're going to score that afternoon, or perhaps tell you it's time you started tucking away the chances again, and you find that sometimes it's a bit of a job becoming sufficiently relaxed.

One ground where I could never feel relaxed was The Den, home of Millwall. I don't know what it's like now, but when I went there with Huddersfield, the dressing-rooms seemed gloomy, the pitch was extremely tight, and the crowd – many of them dockers – seemed to be so hostile that you felt if you started to take liberties with the Lions you would end up being hauled over the parapet. Aldershot was another place I never liked visiting, because there, too, we couldn't seem to get a result. It wasn't a gloomy place, but it was one of those grounds which are open at one end and dipped from the banking on to a road, while the pitch had a slope from one end to the other. It didn't seem to matter if we were playing up the slope or down it, we couldn't put our game together.

Goals? – I've seen a couple of queer ones in my time, and three of the greatest. The first two were scored when I was a Manchester United player – one against United, one for them. Former Tottenham 'keeper Pat Jennings cleared the ball upfield with a mighty thump, on the first occasion, and as Alex Stepney came off his line, the ball bounced once, in front of him, then went over his head and into the net, as he got a touch to it with a couple of fingers.

The second of those goals came in a derby game between Manchester United and Manchester City at Maine-road. I was a spectator for that match, but I can see the ball cleared by the United 'keeper now . . . and suddenly, United forward Alex Dawson was running goalwards, while City 'keeper Bert Trautmann was racing out to intercept. The ball bounced just outside the City penalty area, and Alex and Bert jumped for it together. You saw Alex's hand go up, and touch the ball over the top of Bert's outstretched arms, so that it finished in the net. The referee hadn't seen that flick-on, and he signalled a goal.

Goal No. 3 was Bobby Charlton's glancing header in the 1968 European Cup final against Benfica. Again, I was a spectator, and I saw what appeared to be an innocent cross coming over from John Aston . . . then there was Bobby, who was virtually unknown to head a ball, glancing it home as delicately as you like. One day I must remember to ask him if he scored that goal by design – or by accident.

Goal No. 4 was scored by Malcolm Macdonald, against Leicester City at St James's Park, and it was a remarkable one, indeed. When I arrived at Newcastle, my new team-mates told me what a lethal left foot 'Supermac' had, but this was the first time I saw for myself. Right-back Irving Nattrass made a run down the right flank, and I raced into position to take a pass from him. But suddenly, there was Malcolm, shouting to Irving to put the ball inside to him, and our full-back promptly obliged. As Malcolm was all of 35 yards from goal, everyone expected him to take the ball, push it a few more yards, then have a crack at goal. Instead, he ran straight on to the pass and let fly without a pause. He hit that ball so sweetly with his left foot, and the shot fairly screamed into the net.

And goal No. 5 was another scored by Newcastle, this time started by 'keeper Mike Mahoney, when he threw the ball out to Alan Kennedy. Alan carried it forward about 20 yards and clipped the ball up the line to me. I evaded a challenge from Frank McLintock, got to the by-line and pulled the ball back to the edge of the box, where Mickey Burns was in just the right position to whack it first time into the net. The ball had been played by four Newcastle players, right from our last line of defence . . . and not one player on the opposing side had got a touch to it.

12 Shankly for England!

One England Under-23 cap may not make me an expert on international football, and I must concede that I now appear to be an unlikely candidate for full England international status. Until someone wants an England side with a big, willing workhorse up front, I don't see myself making it as a striker, and until I revert to a midfield role again at club level, I don't imagine anyone would consider me for a berth in this department of the England side. The older you get, the less chance you have of international recognition, too. So, although I still nurse ambitions to play for my country at senior level, I must be realistic and assume that I shall have to number that one Under-23 cap as my sole England souvenir.

I played only once under Sir Alf Ramsey, but what I saw of him impressed me. Especially his preparation and organisation. There was also something about the man which, later in my career, I came to recognise in Gordon Lee. He knew how to wind up players so that they went out and gave him everything. You were playing for Alf Ramsey, as well as for the Under-23 side.

Frankly, I thought Alf was unlucky to lose his job as England's team manager. And I felt a little bit disillusioned by the way he lost it. It has to be admitted that he did not appear to be able to communicate well, other than to his players; and because he was not what you might call a good public-relations man, I felt that this put a great deal of pressure on the powers-that-be in football, when results didn't go right for a spell. The pressure was such that they felt they had to ring the changes. It astonished me, though, because Alf had been the most successful England team manager, and he was recognised as one of the top three international bosses in the world, ranked alongside the men who managed West Germany and Brazil.

Alf was criticised for producing a system which, it was said, was stereotyped; one which, supposedly, didn't entertain the public. It was also claimed in some circles that the Ramsey style of football had had a derogatory effect upon the game in this country as a whole. My answer to that criticism is that the system he devised was good for him as a team manager with Ipswich Town, because it was successful, and it produced a winning pay-off for England when we won the World Cup in 1966. Further, it took us very close to success in Mexico.

All right, so we lost a game after having been two goals up against West Germany. But the players had followed his orders, up to that point, and it was really human error which cost us the match. You could not blame the manager for human error and mistakes out on the field of play which cost two goals. And although we failed to qualify for the 1974 World Cup finals, again it wasn't Ramsey's fault, to my mind. Again, it was a mistake on the field which cost us dearly in Poland, and at Wembley, England did everything right, but the Poles had two men playing out of their skins, in Gorgon and the goalkeeper with the unpronounceable name.

On his record alone, I feel there was no way Alf should have been asked to stand down. But it happened, and his successor was Don Revie, who had built up such a successful club side at Leeds United. Possibly there were people who felt that Leeds hadn't always given every possible help when it came to international calls, in the past, but certainly during Don's tenure as England manager, the international scene received the greatest possible co-operation, if you accept that injuries played a part in hampering the building of a settled World Cup squad.

I think it has to be said that England haven't produced the results, despite the co-operation of the League and the clubs. And I am not disputing for one moment that Don Revie did make every effort to achieve the right results. I'm sure he worked as hard as his predecessor, and was more anxious than anyone to steer England to the finals of the World Cup again.

It's always easy to know what should have been done, with hindsight. Yet I felt when Alf Ramsey left, as I feel today, that England should have gone for a manager who had proved his ability not only to build a club side, but to rebuild one. In short, someone like Bill Shankly. Yes, I would have no compunction about naming a Scot as the manager of England's international team – after all, Wales have enjoyed considerable success with an Englishman, Mike Smith, at the helm.

So far as I can see, the greatest criticism which can be levelled at the England set-up is that drive and motivation appear to have been secondary to the commercial aspects of the situation. That may sound daft, but one of the greatest mistakes, for me, was to increase the money paid to our international players, and to change the playing strip.

The strip was changed to the extent that England's players were advertising the name of a company, and in my view, that tends to denigrate any international pride we might have. The honour of playing for your country must be supreme, above all else, and the money side of the operation should be secondary.

The Scots and the Welsh are much more overt national-
ists than the English, even though they may have changed
their strip to some extent. I'm not suggesting that England's
players are not proud to play for their country, no matter
what kind of shirt they may be wearing; I'm simply saying
that perhaps there was a shift in emphasis which, fun-
damentally, was wrong. When Newcastle United were
returning from a close-season trip to Malta, Tommy Craig,
who has skippered the Scotland Under-23 side several
times, was almost beside himself with anxiety as we flew
home – he couldn't wait to hear how Scotland had fared
in the home international against England at Wembley.
Finally, we had to get the pilot to radio to England for
the result . . . and when Tommy heard that Scotland had
won, he went marching proudly down the gangway of the
aircraft, borrowed a 'tammy' from a youngster, and
paraded around as if he'd come up on the pools. You
see what I mean about overt nationalism . . . we tend to be
much more phlegmatic. And sometimes, maybe, we should
show the flag a bit more than we do.

I'm a supporter of sponsorship in football as a whole,
particularly at club level, but when it comes to the international team, I don't think we should get so involved
in the commercial side. Success in the World Cup brings
its own rewards, in cash, as well as glory.

Like Bill Shankly or Bobby Robson or Brian Clough,
Don Revie has proved himself to be a good motivator, and
a successful club manager. And I'm sure the wish dearest
to his heart was to transmit that success to the international
scene. He might have done so, before he had finished. But I
must be honest and say that he would not have been my
choice, initially. For me, Bill Shankly would have been the
man, if he could have been persuaded to take on the job.

You may argue that a manager is only as good as his

players – in which case, the question arises: are England's players not good enough?

I think we tend to talk about world-class stars as if they were liberally scattered around every club and country bar our own. And that's a wrong assumption to make. You would have great difficulty in picking two world-class teams from players in Europe and South America . . . and you would have to go back a bit, to do so. West Germany has produced Beckenbauer, Muller, Netzer, Seeler; we've seen Cruyff and Neeskens from Holland; Pele, Rivelino, Jairzinho and Gerson from Brazil; Denya and Latto from Poland; and, indeed, Moore, Charlton and Banks from England. Today, I would put forward the names of Kevin Keegan and Ray Clemence as the two world-class players from England.

As for the rest, I think we have sufficient players who ARE good enough – though not world-class stars – to make a successful team. In England terms, we have good players, but there still seems to be something missing . . . and possibly it is the motivation aspect. Successful sides to me seem to be all about team work and understanding, and I believe that in order to get this you have to make up your mind very early which players are going to form your squad.

Then you must stick to those players, perhaps allowing for only one or two changes. Certainly you must create the basis of the side, while accepting that withdrawals through injury can cause problems (and there is no doubt that this did cause Don Revie headaches, at times). I feel that there can be too much experiment, anxious though you may be to give every candidate a chance. You've got to get a settled squad in time, then stick with it, for better or for worse. At least, then, you would have the chance to develop team work and understanding.

It's easy to talk, as I've admitted, and when I look at the many players with claims for international recognition, I realise that picking a 22-man squad is more difficult than it sounds. I also concede that by and large, my ideas on the players I would choose coincided with those of Don Revie. But, as so many armchair managers have done before me, I'll pick 22 men who, I think, would give me a balance between skill and strength, and enable me to permutate and adapt according to the needs of the situation – for I would pick some players for some matches, and other players for different games, depending on the opposition.

My squad would be: Ray Clemence, Peter Shilton; Irving Nattrass, John Gidman, Mick Mills, Phil Thompson, Dave Watson, Kevin Beattie, Emlyn Hughes; Steve Coppell, Martin Dobson, Colin Todd, Brian Talbot, Gerry Francis, Ray Wilkins; Mick Channon, Kevin Keegan, Trevor Whymark, Malcolm Macdonald, Trevor Francis, Dennis Tueart, David Mills.

The departure of Don Revie meant that England had to look for a successor to him, and with this thought in mind, and the job still vacant as I write, I would go for one of three men: Bobby Robson, Bob Paisley or Brian Clough.

Immediately, I begin to reverse the order, because of various factors. Bobby Robson has done an impressive job at Ipswich, but he has yet to rebuild a team, and he has yet to win a major honour. Bob Paisley has won several major honours in quick time, and has partly rebuilt a team, yet each year he is heading towards 60, rather than coming up to 50. Brian Clough has built more than one team, and he has the advantage of youth, as well as experience, on his side. Whatever criticism may have been levelled at 'Cloughy' in the past – and his outspoken comments in newspapers and on television have sometimes made him appear arrogant – he has modified his controversial image distinctly during the past year or two.

He started out with a tough job at Hartlepool, where he went round the pubs and clubs trying to interest fans in the humble little Soccer club. He went to Derby County, and built a team that won the First Division championship. It would be wrong to judge him also on his interludes at Leeds and Brighton, but he turned Nottingham Forest into a First Division club again (and I'm sure my old Newcastle team-mate, Frank Clark, will savour his quick return to the top flight after having been freed from St James's Park). 'Cloughy', for me, has worked a near-miracle at Forest, where his partnership with Peter Taylor has flourished as it did at Derby, and I believe Forest will now make an impact in the First Division.

Frankly, the old image of Brian Clough would have been too much for me; but the new, more mellow 'Cloughy' appeals to me. And whatever one may have thought about his brashness, his at-times abrasive image, it seems to me that the man has managerial talent, and has proved it more than once. So, I feel Brian Clough could be the right man – and I'm sure he would love the chance to prove me right.

Apart from what I have said about various team bosses, one manager I have come to admire very quickly is Manchester City's Tony Book. He has made the transformation from player to manager in a very short time, and generally done it with a great deal of success. He came into League football late as a player, learned a lot and showed he could measure up to the highest standards, and during his short managerial reign he has proved capable of buying shrewdly, organising, delegating and motivating . . . and being unafraid when it comes to a confrontation with players who are big names. He has been prepared to stand up against accepted stars, in order to win what he believes is a necessary battle for the betterment of his club.

I've talked about managers and superstars. There are a few players who, in my book, rate a mention for various qualities. Ian Callaghan, for instance, who is not only a tremendous professional and a team player, but who never shows any pettiness on the field or off it. Even now, I don't think 'Cally' has received the full recognition he deserved. And his former Liverpool team-mate, Peter Thompson, showed character when he left Anfield. It would have been easy for him to stay and carry on receiving good wages, while sitting back in the reserves; it would have been easy for him to fade out of the picture altogether. But he went to Bolton and, when we played them in that marathon Cup duel, he showed a lot of the old magic – and spirit – which first won fame for him. You might have thought you had him beaten, but suddenly he would show you a burst of skill and acceleration which got him out of trouble and set his own side on the attack.

Manchester United's Martin Buchan is another player I admire. Sometimes, maybe, he seems a bit moody; but he's always cool, quick and resourceful, and he organises the players around him. He has a great attitude to the game.

Finally, the two Stevies . . . Coppell and Heighway. Both have been successful in a very rare way, for as I know, it can be difficult to break into football when you have a university background, and to establish yourself in this very professional profession. Each of these players has done more than that. They have earned reputations as being exceptionally good players, particularly Steve

Heighway, whose European experience has helped him to be a very good international player, as well. I believe that he will get better still, and become recognised as a world-class player. And Steve Coppell, with many years ahead of him, could do the same.

But it's not the big names who should command all the attention. I have every admiration for all the players in the Third and Fourth divisions. For them international fame, Cups and League championships are a mirage . . . yet they go out every game and play their hearts out. They may not be in the spotlight on television, yet they always give 100 per cent, even if their wages compare unfavourably with the average industrial pay packet. I'll just select one player who epitomises them all – a striker called Alan Buckley, at Walsall. Season after season, he has plugged away, a regular top scorer in the Third Division. I have always thought he could play in a higher league, and have been surprised that no one has bought him from Walsall. Other players in the lower grades have kept on going, hoping for the lucky break which will give them a chance to make good with a top club; but when it hasn't come, they have continued to do their best for their employers.

The same applies to the workhorses, from First to Fourth Division. Every side has such players – they are too numerous to mention by name. They may not be renowned for exceptional skill or they may not attract the eye of the crowd, possibly because they don't have 'charisma'. But they do an invaluable job for the team, and without them, no side could operate.

13 Soccer Superstition

Honesty is at a premium in football. Gordon Lee and Richard Dinnis are two of the most honest men I've met, but I have also come across a lot of people who can be devious, when it suits their purpose. I'm not pointing an accusing finger at anyone; simply stating a fact of footballing life. You will hear players talking about it being 'time to move on'. They may not say so, but you know their motivation can be summed up in a word: money. They're on the make.

I've played for three clubs, and on none of the occasions when I moved was money the motivating force. Manchester United decided they could do without me; I decided I wasn't going to descend to Division 4 with Huddersfield; and Newcastle offered me a lifeline back to the First Division, at a time when I was prepared to turn my back on the game.

After Gordon Lee had left Newcastle, and there was the question mark against his replacement, the players made it clear they felt Richard Dinnis could do the job. If I had left Newcastle around that time, it wouldn't have been for money – not even a £5,000 'cut' for myself. It would have been because Richard hadn't got the job, and I would have felt somewhat disillusioned. There was talk, indeed, that Gordon Lee would return to Newcastle United, this time with the object of signing myself and Mickey Burns for Everton. It was suggested that Gordon was ready to offer Duncan McKenzie in an exchange deal involving me. I admired, and still admire, Gordon Lee; but, because of the relationship I once had with Ian Greaves, I wouldn't necessarily jump at the chance to join another manager, much as I admired him.

I'm wary now, because I discovered that I had been unwise to commit myself for a long period to a particular club, because of the man in charge. When he left, I was still stuck there, with a good length of my contract to run; and the club wasn't the same without him. I hadn't really weighed up the uncertainty there is in this game, when I signed for Ian Greaves . . . the manager can be on his way, and you're one of the pieces left behind.

When I joined Huddersfield, I signed for the man; when I joined Newcastle United, I signed for myself; and it would be the same if I went anywhere else. At Newcastle, I wasn't playing for a man so much as for the club – although, having said that, it was surprising to me how Gordon Lee could motivate you. What has he got that makes you go out there and run for 90 minutes for him? – I'm not sure of the answer. Mickey Burns and I have talked about this several times, and the best word I can come up with is 'charisma'. It makes players go out and work their guts out for Gordon Lee, and he has obviously got Everton going since he took charge there.

And yet, my admiration for Gordon Lee, a man with a Midlands twang who has this 'charisma', was not the same sort of relationship I had with Ian Greaves. So I'm being totally honest, when I say that even if Gordon Lee had come for me, I wouldn't necessarily have jumped at the chance to play for Everton. Not before assessing everything concerning the club, as well as the man.

I have referred to luck, and superstitions. I won't walk under a ladder, if I can help it. I have a certain routine, when it's time to get ready for the action. I start getting ready about half an hour before kick-off time, and it's always the same order of things . . . taking off my clothes and hanging them on the same peg in the same way, week after week. I believe it's bad luck to start fore-casting results or anticipating events, so I never forecast. If we go on a winning run, I'll stick to wearing the same suit until that run ends. As we go out on the park, it's Geoff Nulty first, then Mike Mahoney, then Alan Kennedy, then me. I couldn't say who follows, although I do know that as we leave the dressing-room, Mickey Burns still hasn't pulled on his shirt, and he does that almost as we are emerging from the tunnel.

Superstition and luck go hand in hand, in most people's eyes. In football, the one is bound up with the other. Footballers resort to luck as an explanation of, or excuse for, the misfortunes that befall them, from time to time. To attempt to avoid ill-luck, they create a belief in super-stition. It applies individually and collectively, and it plays such an important part because mental application is an important factor in football.

A League coach used to say: 'If you're right in mind, then you're right in everything else.' In other words, if you're confident of your ability, then you'll do well on the field. To develop this confidence and (the hardest part) to maintain it, players develop routines. The personal super-stitions may be simple – for example, re-tying bootlaces on the field before the kick-off (as Nobby Stiles used to do), or going out last in line (as Jack Charlton used to do), or putting on a certain boot before the other. These superstitions are followed in order to keep luck on a person's side. Following the routine keeps peace of mind and helps to give confidence. It may seem silly that little things could have such a great effect on some people;

but they do. Jack Charlton gave up the captaincy of Leeds because it meant he had to go out first, rather than last. This change of routine upset him, his mind was unsettled because he wasn't following the superstitions he believed in and which, for him, brought him luck.

The whole team can take on a superstition, too. The successful England World Cup side of 1966 developed such a superstition, for Sir Alf Ramsey was not allowed to go to matches with his track suit on. He kept to this in order not to upset the mental rhythm of his team. And Manchester United had a routine during their run of 1971 which took them five points clear at the top of the First Division table. As the run of results built up, we decreed that a good number of the team came to every game with the same clothes. It became a ritual, a ceremony to luck, to keep it with the team.

It didn't succeed, and it was rapidly ditched when its validity was clearly in question. The routine was out, once its credibility had been exposed.

So footballers are all the time searching for good fortune, and the answer to it. They are in search of success, and who or what brings success to some, and not to others, they do not know. But they attribute it to luck. They must have luck on their side; they must feel lucky. In reverse, a team or an individual can be affected by a feeling of ill-luck. A string of poor results, more often than not due to bad play, but attributed to bad luck, can set a team thinking it is 'jinxed'. So confidence drains away, and the results go from bad to worse.

Confidence and superstition, inextricably entwined, provide the ritual for luck. Luck provides the casual explanation of events. It also provides the excuse. Such is the place of luck in a professional footballer's life. 'If you've got no confidence in your skill, there's no point going on the field.' 'You've got to go out there thinking that you're a bloody great player.'

The player looks to his manager for an injection of confidence. If he feels the manager has confidence in him, it's very likely to have an improving effect upon his own morale. Players who lose confidence in their manager are not likely to have high confidence in themselves, and so their performances will be affected. And yet, for no apparent reason, confidence can be so changeable and sensitive. One day a player can feel full of confidence; the next day he has lost it, and cannot explain why. And the confidence can return as suddenly as it departed.

It isn't always inexplicable, of course. Get in a good tackle or a good shot early in the game, and you can be feeling on top of the world right through the 90 minutes. Give away an own goal, or make an elementary mistake, and you can be afraid to get the ball again. So you go 'hiding'. And your team-mates know it.

There's no hiding place when it comes to local derby games, though, and I've played in a few now. These are the matches where partisan feelings run highest, where the tensions for players and fans alike are the greatest. I have met Newcastle United supporters who have admitted that defeat for the Magpies against Sunderland or Middlesbrough has reduced them to tears of disappointment. There isn't a great deal of difference between derby games in Manchester and the North-East, although I think that perhaps there can be more vicious overtones, and certainly more violence, among the fans who flock to the Manchester derby games. To say the least, each set of supporters is fanatical.

Three derby games stand out in my mind. One was when I played for Manchester United against Manchester City at Maine-road, and City came back to level the score after having gone 3–1 down (I scored in that match). The second was a Newcastle-Middlesbrough tussle at Ayresome Park, when we were losing 3–1 with only a minute to go to the final whistle . . . and we pulled two match-saving goals out of the bag.

It was a shaker for everyone – indeed, a friend of mine for whom I'd got tickets had made his way from the ground believing that Boro' had won 3–1, and it wasn't until I met him later that night that he realised what a grandstand finish he had missed. He took some convincing, even then, that I was telling the truth.

The third derby game which stands out in my mind is one against Sunderland. The first encounter of the season was a bit of a flop – derby games generally come to be classed as dour affairs – perhaps because Sunderland, even then worrying about the peril of relegation, were afraid of making mistakes which could cost them a point, or even two points. The second clash, after Jimmy Adamson had taken over and got the Roker team going, was a totally different affair, magnificent entertainment for the more partisan spectator.

Sunderland's new manager had rung a few changes in the side, and the Roker supporters were hoping and believing that their heroes could stage a miracle recovery (they failed, at the final hurdle) which would enable them to preserve their hard-won First Division status. Sunderland went at us like hornets from the start, and when they drew ahead with two goals in the bag, it seemed they would cruise to victory. But we pulled back, and it finished as a 2–2 draw, so that saved a few blushes on the faces of the fans who supported the Magpies.

There's more atmosphere about a Newcastle-Sunderland derby game than there is about the matches we play against Boro', each season, and this is largely because of the proximity of Tyne and Wear. Some people actually go to watch both Newcastle and Sunderland – although on derby day, they have to come off the fence and root for one team or the other. Mainly, though, there is a distinctive area of support – you're either black and white, or red and white.

I have referred before to the relationship between players and fans, and I think my arrival at Newcastle upset a few, especially when I scored more goals in a season than their hero, Malcolm Macdonald. I know, without anyone telling me, that it wasn't because I had greater skill, or even because I was trying to prove I was better than 'Supermac'. It boiled down to 100 per cent effort, making use of every bit of skill and shooting power that I'd got – and that intangible factor called luck.

It might be thought, from some of my earlier comments about players and supporters, that I've been a little unfair in my generalisations. If so, let me set the record straight, so far as the Geordie fans are concerned. They are among the best in the game – and I include the fanatics of Manchester United, and the Koppites at Liverpool. I realised just how much Newcastle United meant to them when we returned home from the League Cup final of 1976 . . . without the Cup. That, remember, was the second time in three years that Newcastle had been to Wembley, only to return empty-handed, for in 1974, it was Liverpool who carried off the FA Cup.

I was told that when Newcastle got back to the North-East in 1974, they were given a wonderful reception from their supporters, even though, on the day of the game, the Magpies had always looked second-best against the might and power of a confident Liverpool. Frankly, I wondered how the fans would react the second time around . . .

I needn't have worried. We might have been losers, but when we took our salute at St James's Park, the home of Newcastle United, the supporters were there in their thousands – they packed St James's. If I hadn't seen it for myself, I would have found it difficult to believe that a losing team could have been given such a heart-warming reception.

The Geordie fans are not more knowledgeable than those elsewhere, but they are as fervent as any. They will speak their minds, they will criticise, lambast and even upset you with their opinions. But let them get behind you, win them over to your cause and convince them that you're trying your guts out, and they will give you such a volume of support that it cannot fail to inspire you to further effort. I know the Manchester United supporters are rated as being able to see only one colour – red. That is indicative of the way they back their team. But to be blunt, I have to say that I don't think the Manchester United fans would have turned out and given their team the same, overwhelming welcome that the Newcastle supporters did, after we had lost the final battle for the League Cup.

14 We're not Bolshy!

Football is a game which arouses strong passions, provokes arguments, and produces pundits. The game revolves around managers and players, and most people with an interest in the game have their opinions about most aspects of it. For instance, the ability of a man to bring a football under control quickly, glide past opponents using deceptive footwork with the ball still in close control, and pass accurately to a team-mate, is an art appreciated by both players and spectators.

'Given the choice, I'd be a Johnny Giles, or a Bobby Charlton. I'd settle for that. That Gilesie! He just floats about, knocking the ball all over the place. Either foot, no effort – bang-bang-bang. Give him the ball, he wiggles his body and he's off. And chip it? – He can land it on a sixpence! Brilliant, that's what he is.'

I'm still waiting to score my first First Division goal against Ray Clemence of Liverpool. And our rivalry goes back to my reserve days with Manchester United.

In one game, when he was playing for Liverpool reserves, I had eight good chances to tuck the ball away past him – and I didn't find the net once. It wasn't through any lack of ability on my part; I did all the right things, but Ray Clemence anticipated so well, and was so agile, that he stopped me scoring each time through the sheer brilliance of his goalkeeping. Until he came on the scene, Pat Jennings was my No. 1 'keeper, a fellow with tremendous reflexes – he was like a cat when he sprang to snatch the ball to safety.

Both men are good not only at their specialist jobs; they're good at talking their way through a game, and in this way, they maintain their own concentration and keep their back-four men under control, which is a distinct disadvantage, so far as an opposing striker is concerned. I get most pleasure when I know I've stuck away a scoring chance against one of the top goalkeepers in football – my debut goal against Gordon Banks was one instance – because then you feel that you've measured up to all the demands of your own job.

I've mentioned tough defenders, men who play the game hard but fair, and I've talked about the other kind, the players who are known to their fellow-professionals as the 'dirty' guys in the game. I found the lower divisions more physical than the First Division, and the Second (perhaps surprisingly) the toughest of the three in which I've played, from a physical point of view. I came up against one defender during my days in the lower divisions, and every time the ball came near me he seemed about to launch me into space. And right the way through the game, he never exchanged one word with me. Oddly enough, as a person off the field, I found that I could quite like him.

Manchester City manager Tony Book had some hard words to say about one of his players, my former Manchester United team-mate, Brian Kidd, being victimised through what has become known as 'trial by television'. Indeed, the City manager claimed that it could have cost his team the title, for after television had spotlighted an incident in a game involving 'Kiddo', his manager felt he never quite managed to instil the same sharpness or aggression into his play again that season, and his scoring rate slackened off.

Jimmy Hill was the man who incurred the wrath of Tony Book, because he highlighted the match incident on TV, and expressed his comments in a manner which was not flattering to City or to 'Kiddo'. I don't pretend that I should sit in judgement on that particular incident, but I do know what I feel about Jimmy being critical on television. Quite simply, I do not like it.

In the past two or three years, there has been a great deal of argument about the so-called freedom of contract which the players sought. I happen to be a member of the Professional Footballers Association committee, so I can speak with a fair amount of authority on this thorny question and, for a start, I would like to emphasise that in many instances, our aims and demands were not properly understood. In fact, I believe it would be right to say that not all the clubs really realised what would be involved, and perhaps this is why there were clubs which did their damnedest to postpone, if not ward off altogether, what they called 'the evil days'.

So let us take a realistic look at the situation as it has existed for years. Since the abolition of the maximum wage, there has been a great deal of misrepresentation and misunderstanding of the market situation of the professional footballer. The 'stars' among the players have received a lot of publicity about life styles and earnings, but they are not representative of the market situation as a whole.

The market situation is made up of a number of factors, such as wages, bonuses, the Players' Provident Fund, transfer fees, signing-on fees, and other 'perks'. It is further complicated by the fact that not all the same factors apply to all players. For example, the provident-fund payments cover only those players whose earnings have not reached £3,000 a year. 'Perks' such as television appearances, and payment for these, are much more likely to be earned by a handful of 'star' players, so no hard-and-fast ruling can be given on the market situation of any one player, because it can vary so much from the general situation.

Basic wages vary, even between players at the same club; so do bonuses for success, or for appearances in the first team. For the highest-paid players in the top level of the industry (and professional football IS an industry), one or two clubs run pension schemes, but the players involved pay into these, and the sums can be pretty high, if the maturing date is the player's 35th birthday. For a player unlucky enough to have his career ended by injury, there is a payment of £750, and all players receive such a sum, although there are more fortunate individuals (if you can say that about anyone who loses his livelihood through injury) who might receive payments from his club, or a testimonial match. But there are no guarantees in this respect – a player has to rely on the goodwill of his club, so far as the latter payments are concerned.

More often than not, the public believes that footballers are well paid, collectively and that by the time they retire they will have enough to live comfortably for the rest of their lives. This thinking is based on reports of star players having received many thousands of pounds from a testimonial match. So some players in the 'elite' bracket do wind up rich – though even a testimonial rake-off is not necessarily sacrosanct, so far as the tax-man is concerned.

The vast majority of professional footballers certainly would not go along with the general thinking of the public, because they know how much is in their wage packet, and they know that their career will be over, when others in industry have not yet reached their earning peak. Steve Heighway, talking about players' pay – and he is generally regarded as being one of the top players in the game, at a top club – has suggested that the professional footballer has a claim for being regarded as a 'special case', from a tax point of view. You can earn high wages and big bonuses over a short period of time – but the tax man takes a hefty chunk of that money, and it leaves only the 'thin end' to be saved for the time you have to go out of the game and earn a living at something else, around the age of 35.

In signing a contract, a player becomes severely restricted in his freedom, and in a large number of respects is under the control of the club, the Football League and the Football Association. This control may be benevolent, but the iron hand is undoubtedly there, should the club, the League or the FA wish to use it. For serious offences of misconduct, the club can rescind a player's contract; for minor infringements, it has the right to suspend a player and fine him not more than the sum of two weeks' wages.

In recent years, the interests of the players have become more widely recognised, largely through the efforts of the Professional Footballers Association. And the PFA believes that 'freedom of contract' will make for better relations all round. When professionalism was eventually accepted in the game, the status of players was still that of 'servants' to the 'masters' who ran the club. The situation has improved enormously, but now and again, you still sense a hint of the traditional attitudes towards the professional player.

This is reflected in the length of time it has taken the governing bodies of football to reach a decision to abandon the distinction between amateur and professional players. The decision did not come into effect until season 1974–75, from which time all footballers became known as players . . . but this was still some time after similar changes were undertaken by the governing bodies of tennis and cricket. The Chester Committee report found this anachronistic attitude intolerable, and severely reprimanded the FA.

'This discrimination against those who have earned their money by playing the game is an unjustified slur upon a great many people who have much to offer the administration of the game.'

The Professional Footballers Association is, in effect, the players' union. As such, it has a role 'to negotiate the conditions for the players, and to protect the players' interests at all times.' In fulfilling this role, the PFA operates an accident scheme, a provident fund, an education scheme, and provides free legal advice and assistance in any matter arising from contracts. The PFA also makes available the facility of professional accountants, if players wish to use such a service.

In its negotiations on behalf of the players, the PFA does regard itself as militant, and there is no doubt that in recent years the League and the FA have taken the players' union increasingly seriously. Strike action has been threatened twice in PFA history, and there was talk of similar action, during the much-delayed and disputed negotiations concerning freedom of contract, but the PFA, without a shadow of doubt, prefers to get round the table and negotiate.

The PFA has been militant. It has gone into the courts on four occasions. At the time the PFA last went to court, its total assets were £14,000, and these included the benevolent fund, the accident fund and the general fund. Had the PFA lost that action, it would have been in debt to the tune of £25,000. In short, it would have been bankrupt.

The PFA believes that strike action is not the right

F

way, when there are correct procedural processes. Strike action, it was conceded, 'would cripple more than half the clubs.' Attendances would fall, as a result. 'We would ruin the game, if we went on strike . . . strikes are not the answer to anything.' But 'if you could get into the court and be prepared to speculate your finances in order to establish the right of your members, you could go far.' And the PFA, having gone into the courts and won its case, has gone far.

In seeking freedom of contract, the PFA has done no more than seek parity with other working groups. The association, quite simply, wanted to see players free to move at the end of their contracts. The PFA believed freedom would improve the relationship 100 per cent at club level. 'The clubs would no longer be gaffers . . . a better relationship would take place overnight. Players would be treated like human beings.'

There are roughly 2,500 professional footballers in England and Wales, and the PFA represents about 96 per cent of them. There is not a club where the association is not represented, and at each club his role is to collect the dues and distribute any information that comes to him for the members' benefit.

The long-serving secretary of the PFA is Cliff Lloyd, a former player. Jimmy Hill, whom I have mentioned in another context earlier, is a former chairman of the association. Terry Neill, now managing Arsenal, was also chairman at one time, and Derek Dougan later became the chairman.

The relationship of the PFA to individual clubs has been mixed, over the years. Sometimes clubs have sought advice or information from the PFA; sometimes the atmosphere has been hostile, not least when the association has been defending the rights of the players. The PFA, for sure, is recognised by all clubs as the rightful representative of the players, possibly because, in the past, it has not always come down on the side of a player in dispute with his club.

There are cases where a player is obviously in the wrong, and in such a case, the PFA will advise the player to withdraw his protest. On the other hand, if the association feels a club is mistreating a player, the club knows it is in for a fight. Everyone knows a case where a manager for one reason or another has found some player to be of no value to the club, not infrequently when the manager himself is new to the club. In such cases, the player may well feel himself to be victimised, and if so, he may approach the PFA for support: PFA mediation in such cases can be powerful enough to induce the club to change its line.

When it comes to disciplinary proceedings, the PFA may be called on by a player or a club to give assistance, even if it is merely to help get witnesses to appear. The witnesses, of course, are usually the players who were involved in the incident leading to the need for a hearing, and the problem for the PFA is that it can only ask a player (or players) if he (or they) will assist another player in his appeal. Most times there is a positive response; but there are occasions when the potential witness feels he is the aggrieved party, as when a player refused to appear, on the grounds that 'he (the accused player) was an effing liar, and what's more, I've got a black eye to prove it.'

These days, managers are getting as ruthless with players as directors are with managers, claims the association. 'Half a loaf is better than none, and it does not matter what goes on on the field; if he (the manager) gets one point out of the game, he is delighted. There is

too much hypocrisy in the game.' Well, I said at the start
of the previous chapter that few people in football were
totally honest. It's not the game that is wrong; it's the
people in it – or, rather, the attitudes of the people in it.
And on the question of discipline and morality, the PFA
is very critical not only of clubs, but of players.

The PFA has long held that until everyone was honest,
and stopped appealing on behalf of players merely to have
them available for an important match, the situation would
not improve. There have been signs in recent seasons that
clubs are seeing the light, and fining players for misconduct on the field, but naturally, no one ever expects
to see the day when we shall have perfection. But since
the Union of professional Footballers was pioneered by
the players of Manchester United at a meeting held in
Manchester in January, 1898, the players have helped
to improve things as much as anyone else.

Over the years, there have been bubblings of discon-
tent, and in 1960 came the eruption, when negotiations
between the PFA and the Football League broke down,
and eventually, the players gave notice of strike action, the
deadline being set for January 21, 1961. Clubs planned to
play their games using amateur players, but after Ministry
of Labour intervention, they offered to abolish the
maximum-wage restriction, but would not concede on the
retain-and-transfer clauses, and the players rejected the
move.

Three days before the players were due to strike, agreement was reached on abolishing the maximum wage and
on altering the player's contract, but the League decided
to go back on its agreement, and apply the retain-and-
transfer system. So, two years after having reached agreement, the PFA was back in dispute with the League, and
this time the setting was the High Court.

George Eastham, a Newcastle United player, had asked for a transfer; his request had been refused, and he was placed on the retained list. Having gone through the appeal system laid down by the League, Eastham decided to take legal action, after he had not received satisfaction, in his opinion. Before the High Court action was concluded, he had been transfered to Arsenal, but the legal process went on, and judgement was given in favour of the player. This ended another area of conflict, but the freedom-of-contract problem remained, and several years were spent thrashing that matter out.

The Eastham judgement had an almost immediate effect upon the status of players. They were at last beginning to shake off the shackles of the master-servant relationship, and were no longer wholly in the hands of clubs, to be manipulated at will.

When it came to the freedom-of-contract issue, there were people who suggested that it would be all right for the favoured few, the players who had made their names and could be sure of becoming targets for the big clubs. But what about the 'poor bloody infantry' – the majority of footballers who could not claim star billing or, therefore, star treatment?

I have enjoyed my involvement as a representative of the PFA, and it has added to my experience of life in professional football. The game isn't ALL about what happens during the 90 minutes of action on the park, and I like to feel I am contributing to the welfare of the players off the field. My own experience of having played in three of the four divisions of the Football League helps me in this respect, I feel.

Clubs may regard the PFA as a bloody nuisance, because – apart from anything else – it has helped to change the status of the players. Now, they won't accept what was once their traditional place in the football world, the bottom rung of the social ladder. But so far as the players in the lower divisions feeling that the freedom issue is 'all for the big boys of the top clubs', I say just as firmly that this is not the case.

Having been in the lower divisions myself, I know what it's like not to breathe the air at the top, and I would never agree to any action which I thought would be detrimental to the players in the lower divisions. Who am I to stand up and say: 'Sorry, mate . . . you're down the road . . . get looking for another job.' I sincerely believe the PFA has acted all along in the best interests of all its members, and I've been in a position where I could see the work being done.

I feel that the clubs, by and large, have been too suspicious of what it would all mean, that in some instances they have been panicked and not got to grips with what the situation entails. Let's face it, you cannot accuse a union of being 'bolshy' when, in fact, there have been only three major changes in the industrial relations in that industry (professional football) in 90 years. Compare that with all the changes that have taken place in other industries.

15 Football's Future

During the past few years of negotiations over freedom of contract for professional footballers, relations between the Football League and the PFA have improved considerably. Certainly this has been the case so far as the PFA and League Management Committee have been concerned. There were people at the top in club boardrooms who said at first that the players would gain freedom only over their bodies. Peter Swales, chairman of Manchester City, was against freedom, in the first place; so was Bob Lord, the chairman of Burnley. The former is also an FA councillor, the latter a vice-president of the Football League, so each wields considerable influence. But both these men, in the end, came to the conclusion that freedom of contract was inevitable. And they worked hard to help bring about implementation of the new deal.

Some clubs, however, were against the 'freedom' idea from the start, and they maintained their views over a considerable period of time. They were mostly from the Midlands area, and they formed a powerful force when they banded together to contest the proposals.

Their fears included, among other things, the prospect of players 'hawking' themselves around to the highest bidders, and they argued that the proposals concerning compensation for clubs were not 'on'. Among these 'rebel' clubs, who seemed determined to defy the management committee to the bitter end, were **Stoke City, Coventry**

City, Birmingham City, Wolves, West Brom and Aston Villa. Other clubs were also believed to be in sympathy with them, and for many months the issue of freedom of contract was delicately balanced, as the League Management Committee found its proposals thwarted, to the extent that meetings of the clubs were shelved more than once, as the lobbying for support continued. It took a long, long time as the League sought to find a solution acceptable to the clubs generally, and during that time, the patience of the players began to wear thin.

It is true that there was talk of strike action if the new deal did not go through for the start of season 1977–78, but all the way along the line, the PFA tried its utmost to persuade the players that patience was not only a virtue; it was of paramount importance. For the battle this time was not so much between PFA and the League; it was between the clubs themselves. And in the end, it was hoped patience would prevail.

The future of professional football is not bound up solely with the freedom-of-contract issue, however. There are other items which will have to be closely watched – and acted upon – if this great national game of ours is to continue as a source of entertainment for millions of people. The influx of big money has put a premium on success – that cannot be denied. It has led to the development of lowering standards of ethics both by managers and players.

There is so much pressure on players and managers that a win-at-all-costs attitude has certainly crept into the game. This has brought defensive football, and 'professional' and violent play.

This development, along with violence on the terraces and among travelling spectators, has been one factor that has led to a decrease in attendances at matches. It is necessary – indeed, unavoidable – if the game is to continue with any prosperity at all that there should be a moral change in the attitude of managers and players – more shouts of 'Play football!', and fewer demands to 'break his effing leg!'

More money must be pumped into the game, and perhaps the football pools companies have the answer to this. Before very long, someone will be acclaimed as the first person to win a million pounds for having found eight score-draws on the coupon. That money could ruin the life of the person who wins it; but only a small portion of it could mean the difference between life and death for a football club.

Football, traditionally, has been a reasonably cheap form of entertainment. With the increased demands for money, success and expenditure by clubs, the gate receipts have not kept in step. But, unfortunately, if the imbalance should be reversed, the only thing that is likely to happen is that more people will be forced away from the game.

In the next 10 years, given the present economic situation, a reduction in the number of clubs seems inevitable, and this will probably come in stages, starting with regionalisation, then more part-time players; then clubs dropping out of the League. The vast majority of clubs are in the red, and I have often wondered how long people such as directors, who stand as guarantors, and creditors, are going to wait before shouting 'Time up.'

We have seen in recent seasons how some clubs have been in desperate straits . . . Newport County, Stockport County, Workington, Southport, Portsmouth, even Chelsea, who are now back in the First Division. One wonders if they could have stood another season in Division 2.

The problem of clubs being hard-up is not new, but because of the economic uncertainty nation-wide regarding business and so on, there may be a situation soon when the creditors are going to want their money out in order to fulfil their own obligations.

The possibility of a super-league has been discussed more than once, over the past decade. To me, a super-league seems remote. British spectators get plenty of chance to see foreign teams because of the number of European competitions (it would be interesting to learn, also, the number of people who stayed up to watch the European Cup-winners Cup final on television between Anderlecht and SV Hamburg, in the spring of 1976 – in short, do we WANT to see foreign teams, except when they are in direct competition with our own clubs?).

I believe it is extremely unlikely that foreign clubs and our own clubs would desert their own national leagues to band together and form a super-league, because competition is the lifeblood of the game, and there must be some sort of promotion and relegation; a carrot dangled in front of clubs for success, albeit a penalty clause for failure.

Increased expenditure and the decline in attendances is going to continue, despite the optimistic forecasts of some people, and the English division which has suffered most from falling gates in recent years has been the First . . . where, you would fondly imagine, the greatest attraction would lie. What would the big clubs gain, by joining a super-league? – Extra support – for a time. Extra expense – all the time. And a gradual lessening of interest, as the opposing sides became commonplace, after the initial novelty of the thing.

I do not want to play the part of the pessimist. I have said I am a fatalist, but I also try to be an optimist, for that is my nature. I also believe that my experience – my personal experiences – in professional football have taught me quite a bit about the game, and the people in the game. I spent three years researching material for a 60,000-word thesis I wrote on the game for my master's degree at Manchester University (incidentally, a high-ranking official, having read the thesis, said that while he could see nothing wrong with the document, he could not guarantee that members of the FA Council would think the same . . . and that publication of my thesis might be construed as de-nigrating my fellow-professionals).

The thought occurred to me at the time that football doesn't much like to see itself in the mirror – especially if the self-examination is going to be conducted in public. But perhaps if we all looked in the mirror a bit more, and took a constructive attitude, the process would prove less painful than many people fear. The face of football shows up the belmishes; but self-examination need not be destructive.

A Danish sports journalist to whom I talked not so long ago pondered why English club football was so successful in Europe, while our national team struggled to make an impact. You will recall that at Wembley, in recent inter-national matches, there have been occasions when our players have heard the taunts of 'What a load of rubbish!' And they have been the target for the abuse.

People who regard themselves as experts on the game have criticised us for being far behind the Continentals in skill, technique and general organisation. And we appear at times to take a perverse sort of pleasure in denigrating ourselves. Maybe it's a good, old-fashioned English custom.

Yet, as I said, English clubs command the respect of their rivals in Europe, and perhaps one of our major flaws is that we pronounce judgement – mistakenly – on what the team put out by England achieves, or fails to achieve. People may look on the England team and deride its performances, at times, while they point to the Dutch and West Germans as the epitome of all that is right with the game – yet foreign clubs have been known to come to these shores and sign our players. So can we be all that bad?

Our mistake is that we assume crack foreign international

sides reflect the state of club football in their respective countries, and while it may be hammering a theme, I maintain, as do many other people, that our First Division is still the best, for all-round strength, skill and achievement. In this country, the football fans haven't shown any enthusiasm for 'possession' football, yet we don't present it in a form anywhere near as strong as the Continentals do. Those who crave for the transplantation of the Continental approach over here would soon have a change of heart . . . they simply wouldn't stand for it.

Whether the influx of English players such as Kevin Keegan, Roger Davies and others will have its effect on European football remains to be seen. I believe that in the next couple of years, the Continentals will come for more of our star players, and that after that there could well be a steady flow of what you might call the 'bread-and-butter' footballers across the Channel. The tax system here doesn't encourage people to stay in England, if they can earn far more – and keep far more in their pockets – by working in Europe. So our big clubs may well begin to feel the draught, and the rest will follow as a natural progression. Given the chance, I would go abroad, if it meant obtaining financial security for the rest of my life.

Remember that a player's career ends at a time when his overheads are likely to be increasing – the kids will need educating, the mortgage must still be paid, and the household bills will not get less. But the player's wage, assuming he finds a job outside the game, will go down. And even though a footballer may earn a lot of money during his playing career, he finds it impossible to save much for the future, because of the tax system. So he has to accept a likely decline in his living standards (when his playing career ends) at a time when other people are looking for promotion in their jobs. Can you blame a player if, with his best two or three years in front of him, he decides to up-root and stick it out in a European city because he can earn far greater rewards than with a top First Division club over here? – I can't.

When SV Hamburg signed Kevin Keegan, Liverpool manager Bob Paisley was warning that other English stars could follow, and it was suggested that players going abroad might be banned from continuing to play for England. Undoubtedly there is a danger that our inter-national side would be denuded of some of its best foot-ballers; and there have been problems on the Continent already where a club has refused to release a man to play for his country. I believe that FIFA will have to take action, in this respect, get a clear understanding that any player signing for a foreign club must be released to play for his country in competitive international matches, should he be selected.

At the same time, I also believe that if the European continent poses a threat, the American Soccer scene pre-sents an even bigger one. The game in the US is still in its infancy, but already American clubs have been to England to sign not the star players, but many of the 'bread-and-butter' men. Players from all divisions have already sampled Soccer in America, and the traffic is certain to increase. A lot of players could be crossing the Atlantic.

I have mentioned the pressures on people in the game to achieve success, and I know there are a lot of things wrong with our football – at the bottom end of the scale, as well as at the top. For instance, I think we should take another look at the system under which clubs can sign 'associated' schoolboys. I think that, with the headmaster's and parents' consent, a boy should be allowed to sign for a professional club at the age of 13, but that his pro-gress should be reviewed year by year, and that his contract should be year by year. I also believe that if, at the end of 12 months, the lad is unhappy at a club or doesn't believe he's been getting proper coaching or treatment, he should be allowed to leave and, if he wishes, to join another club. I further believe that while he is attached to a club, there should be a compulsory training scheme which ensures that he does receive a grounding in another field, whether it be academic or practical, so that if football failed to give him a career, or if he failed to achieve success, he could switch to another job before he signed apprentice at the age of 16.

I've mentioned coaching, and in many ways, the attitude to coaches isn't right. I must admit I'm a bit sceptical about coaching certificates, because a slip of paper doesn't mean a man is good at this specialist job. Equally, I'm sceptical of those who claim you cannot be a good coach unless you have been a professional footballer. Mike Smith has proved the point that if you have a real feel for the game, and can put your message across, you will be accepted by the professionals AND you will do well. An economics degree doesn't qualify anyone to be Chancellor of the Exchequer; but if a man is a financial genuis, he might be a success as Chancellor, even without the degree. And the same argument applies to coaching, for me. By the same token, some coaches get coaching a bad name, because they have the slip of paper but not the right qualities to do the job.

We have to live with the realities of the situation, too. I acknowledge this. Regularly, we hear the plea that teams should go out and entertain, rather than putting a blanket of negative play upon a game. Yet how many prizes do you get for entertainment value? The craving for success – for victory at all costs – is the dominant factor; or, to put it another way, the fear of losing (and thus being labelled a failure) casts its shadow over all. So if we genuinely want to put the emphasis on entertaining, we have to re-move the element of fear.

One way of doing this would be to create a system where-by a manager doesn't get the bullet at the drop of a director's hat. Another way to encourage more positive football would be to readjust the points system, with three points for an away win, instead of two.

It may seem like heresy especially since I have referred to the competition element earlier in this chapter, but there might be something to be said for revising the system of promotion and relegation . . . or even considering scrap-ping relegation for a trial period of three or fours years. Cer-tainly, I feel that the size of each division must be reduced.

For years, the players in our leagues have been asked to compete at the highest level for too often and too long – in short, they have been asked to play too many matches. Liverpool's dilemma was a case in point, when they were going for a treble. They had to contend with injuries, with 42 League games, and with battling their way through to the finals of the FA Cup and European Cup. Oh, yes – they did take part in the League Cup, as well. During the last month of their season, they were playing a game every three days, and when they went to Rome for the final of the European Cup, they had played 60 matches (and lost only 11), while their opponents, Borussia Moenchengladbach had played 44 (and lost 10). The attitudes of players, coaches and managers may play a considerable part in weakening the entertainment value of the show, but the wear and tear on players takes its toll, as well. In no uncertain fashion. And Liverpool deserve the highest credit for the display they gave in Rome, as well as for winning the European Cup.

I've referred more than once to the need for greater communication, and I believe this involves getting every single one of football's leading bodies – League, FA, PFA

AND referees – to talk to each other . . . not only more often, but more openly. Our attitudes have been 19th-century for too long, and discussion is vital, because only through discussion can you arrive at understanding. And if you don't understand what the other guy is trying to do, or what he needs, then you cannot hope to make real progress. Despite the opposition there was by some clubs to freedom of contract, at least they and the players had been talking, trying to reach understanding. So we have shown that while there is a great deal to think about, much to learn and to be done, there is much for which we can still hope.

In this book, I have tried to present a balanced view, to show the blacks, the whites and the shades of grey. I have tried not to knock the game which brings me a living, but I have also endeavoured not to put on the blinkers, because it would be folly to pretend that in professional football, you have the best of all possible worlds all the time. There are high spots and low points, comedies and tragedies played out on the park and behind the scenes. And my own experience has confirmed this, time and again.

Looking back on my own career, and giving a personal view of what has happened to me, I shall finish by answering a question my co-writer asked me: 'Given your time over, and knowing what you know now, would you make the same choice again?' The answer is short, simple and very much to the point. I'd do it all, right the way through, and have no regrets. Football has taught me a lot; I hope and believe I have contributed something to the game.

This book has had its serious notes, perhaps an amusing story or two, and I have used the 'industrial' language of the pro., on occasion. It's basically a story which applies to most professional footballers, and one thing I can say, without fear of contradiction is this: what I have related is simply football . . . inside-out.